AF600678

The Phonology of Contrast

Advances in Optimality Theory

Series Editors: Vieri Samek-Lodovici, *University College London*, and Armin Mester, *University of California at Santa Cruz*

Optimality Theory is an exciting new approach to linguistic analysis that originated in phonology but was soon taken up in syntax, morphology, and other fields of linguistics. Optimality Theory presents a clear vision of the universal properties underlying the vast surface typological variety in the world's languages. Cross-linguistic differences once relegated to idiosyncratic language-specific rules can now be understood as the result of different priority rankings among universal, but violable constraints on grammar.

Advances in Optimality Theory is designed to stimulate and promote research in this provocative new framework. It will provide a central outlet for the best new work by both established and younger scholars in this rapidly moving field. The series includes studies with a broad typological focus, studies dedicated to the detailed analysis of individual languages, and studies on the nature of Optimality Theory itself. The series publishes theoretical work in the form of monographs and coherent edited collections as well as pedagogical texts and reference texts that promote the dissemination of Optimality Theory.

Consultant Board

The Phonology of Contrast

Anna Łubowicz

Published by Equinox Publishing Ltd.

UK: Unit S3, Kelham House, 3 Lancaster Street, Sheffield S3 8AF
USA: ISD, 70 Enterprise Drive, Bristol, CT 06010

www.equinoxpub.com

First published in 2012

ISBN: 978-1-84553-416-5 (hardcover)

British Library Cataloguing-in-Publication Data
A catalogue record for this book is available from the British Library.

Library of Congress Cataloging-in-Publication Data
Lubowicz, Anna.
The phonology of contrast / Anna Lubowicz.
p. cm.—(Advances in optimality theory)
Includes bibliographical references and index.
ISBN 978-1-84553-416-5 (hb) 1. Minimimal pair (Linguistics) I. Title.
P128.M56L83 2010
415—dc22
2009021282

Typeset by JS Typesetting Ltd, Porthcawl, Mid Glamorgan
Printed and bound in the UK by MPG Books Group.

Contents

Acknowledgments

This book represents my research on contrast in phonology and phonology–morphology interface. This line of research grew out of my 2003 dissertation from the University of Massachusetts at Amherst. While the main thesis did not change, this book contains many significant new ideas and extensions. I have refined the model of contrast proposed in my earlier work and set the manuscript in a broader context of other work on contrast. In addition, I have extended the discussion of the role of contrast to morphological contrast as well as discussed more data in the area of phonological contrast.

This project began when I was a graduate student at the University of Massachusetts. I would like to thank my Ph.D. guidance committee from the University of Massachusetts and Rutgers University, John McCarthy, Alan Prince, Lisa Selkirk, John Kingston, and Robert Rothstein. I would also like to thank my colleagues and students at the University of Minnesota and the University of Southern California: Dani Byrd, Louis Goldstein, Jeanette Gundel, Alex Jaker, Elsi Kaiser, Ben Munson, Sarah Ouwayda, Daylen Riggs, Meghan Sensenbach, Hooi-Ling Soh, Hidekazu Tanaka, Rachel Walker, and Jean-Roger Vergnaud. I am also grateful to participants of numerous conferences and workshops where this work was presented, including Eric Bakovic, Malgosia Cavar, Dan Dinnsen, Bruce Hayes, Larry Hyman, Junko Ito, Marc van Oostendorp, Jaye Padgett, Jerzy Rubach, Donca Steriade, Bruce Tesar, Colin Wilson, and Kie Zuraw. I would also like to thank Brett Borchardt, Andries Coetzee, Maria Gouskova, and Nicole Nelson for reading various drafts of this work.

Finally, I would like to thank the series editors at Equinox, Armin Mester and Ellen Woolford, for their continuous support and encouragement, the team at Equinox, Janet Joyce, Valerie Hall, Gina Mance, Hamish Ironside, Kate Williams, and Judy Napper, for technical expertise and handling production of this work, and the reviewers for excellent comments and suggestions.

This book is dedicated to my daughters, Julia Aleksandra and Kate Helena Borchardt, and my husband, Brett Borchardt.

1 Introduction

1.1 What this book is about

This book provides a formal theory of contrast called PC theory (for "preserve contrast") (Łubowicz 2003, 2007). The proposal is couched within a framework of Optimality Theory (hereafter OT) (Prince and Smolensky 1993/2004).

Much current research in phonology and morphology investigates the role of contrast. Contrast has been used to account for segmental inventories (Bradley 2001, Flemming 1995, 1996, 2004, Padgett 1997, 2001), historical change (Ito and Mester 2004, 2007, Padgett 2000, 2003, Padgett and Zygis 2007, Parrell 2007, Sanders 2003), segmental complexity (Avery *et al.* 2008, Dresher 2003, Dresher *et al.* 1994, Rice and Avery 1993), feature co-occurrence restrictions (Cote 2000), morphological processes (Crosswhite 1997/1999, Horwood 2001, Jaker 2006, Kenstowicz 1996, 2005, Kurisu 1998, Łubowicz 2007, Rebrus and Törkenczy 2005, Steriade 1997, 2000, Urbanczyk 1998, 1999), stress-epenthesis interaction (Łubowicz 2003), quantitative adjustments (Riggs 2008), tonal and accentual phenomena (Alderete 2001a, 2001b), and chain shift mappings (Barrie 2006, Hsieh 2005, Łubowicz 2003, 2004, Tessier 2004). Contrast has also been investigated in the areas of syntax and semantics (Flack 2007, Liao 2007). Earlier work on contrast includes Firthian linguistics (Firth 1957, Mitchell 1975) and structuralist linguistics (Bloomfield 1984, Martinet 1952, Saussure 1983, Trubetzkoy 1971). This book contributes to the research on contrast by providing a framework of contrast and investigating its empirical coverage.

The proposal developed in this book finds its inspiration in the work on opacity and recoverability in the 1970s. The main idea expressed in those works is that input representations should be recoverable from the surface forms in the language, and opaque phonological processes increase recoverability (see Donegan and Stampe 1979, Gussmann 1976, Hualde 1990, Kaye 1974, 1975, and Kisseberth 1976). The theory of contrast developed in this book, called PC theory, follows this insightful observation about opaque phonological processes and incorporates it into a framework of rankable and violable constraints.

The core observation is that chain shifts and other opaque phonological processes involve *contrast transformation* where a given underlying contrast is preserved on the surface but manifested as a different surface contrast. This is at the cost of neutralizing some other contrast in the grammar. PC theory provides a framework to capture this observation formally.

The key argument is that contrast exists as a formal principle in the grammar which in the framework of OT is formalized as a family of rankable and violable constraints on preserving contrasts, called PC constraints. PC constraints interact with each other and with conflicting markedness constraints, resulting in various patterns of preservation and/or neutralization of contrasts. The interaction of contrast and markedness determines many patterns of contrast preservation in the language, but an important observation made in this work is that to effectively evaluate contrast, it is necessary to include generalized faithfulness constraints in the theory (Chapter 2). Generalized faithfulness constraints are also formulated as recoverability in cases of contrast displacement (Chapters 3 and 4).

In this proposal, contrast is evaluated over a finite set of input–output mappings, called a scenario. An algorithm for how to generate a scenario will be proposed (Chapter 2). A scenario represents various interplays of contrast and the optimal scenario is chosen by the rankable and violable constraints.

As will be discussed, PC theory has far-reaching consequences. One of the key predictions is that in this framework, contrast together with markedness can trigger a phonological process. This has implications for the typology of chain shifts, stress-epenthesis interaction and allomorphy. It also provides a uniform analysis of opaque and transparent phonological processes without additional mechanisms required. Implications of the proposal will be discussed and compared with alternatives.

1.2 Key questions

The key question that will be addressed in this book is where contrast fits into the grammar: is contrast a derivative of a phonological system or a primitive stated as a separate principle in the grammar? Based on evidence from phonology and morphophonology, this book will argue that contrast exists as an imperative in a phonological system and will develop a framework of contrast called PC theory.

There are many approaches where contrast is not a separate principle of the grammar but falls out from other components of the grammar. In generative phonology (Chomsky and Halle 1968), the presence or absence of contrast directly correlates with the presence or absence of a phonological rule. Contrast is neutralized when a phonological rule applies. Contrast is preserved when a phonological rule does not apply. This is illustrated below.

(1-1) Rule-based analysis of final devoicing

a. Language with final devoicing (e.g. Polish)

Input	/bug/ ‘god’	/buk/ ‘beech’
Final devoicing	buk	n/a
Output	[buk]	[buk]

b. Language without final devoicing (e.g. English)

Input	/bæg/ ‘bag’	/bæk/ ‘back’
No rule of final devoicing	n/a	n/a
Output	[bæg]	[bæk]

In the language with a final devoicing rule (see (1-1a)), the voicing contrast is neutralized in word-final position. In the language with no rule of final devoicing (see (1-1b)), the voicing contrast is preserved.

Similarly, in OT contrast follows from the interaction of faithfulness and markedness constraints. When faithfulness outranks conflicting markedness, contrast is preserved. With the opposite ranking, contrast is neutralized. Consider final devoicing in standard OT. When markedness against voiced obstruents word-finally outranks conflicting faithfulness, final devoicing takes place and the voicing contrast is neutralized. With the opposite ranking, there is no devoicing and the voicing contrast is preserved. The following tableaux illustrate the two cases: a language with final devoicing in (1-2) and without devoicing in (1-3). In each case, two types of inputs are considered: one with a voiced obstruent syllable-finally and one with a voiceless obstruent in the same position.

(1-2) Final devoicing (cf. (1-1a))

		/bu**g**/	*VOICEDOBS]$_\sigma$	IDENT(voice)
a.	☞	bu**k**		*
b.		bu**g**	*!	

		/bu**k**/	*VOICEDOBS]$_\sigma$	IDENT(voice)
c.	☞	bu**k**		
d.		bu**g**	*!	*

(1-3) No final devoicing (cf. (1-1b))[1]

		/bæ**g**/	IDENT(voice)	*VOICEDOBS]$_\sigma$
a.		bæ**k**	*!	
b.	☞	bæ**g**		*

		/bæ**k**/	IDENT(voice)	*VOICEDOBS]$_\sigma$
c.	☞	bæ**k**		
d.		bæ**g**	*!	*

Let us consider forms with a voiced obstruent word-finally in both languages. Those are the top tableaux in each case, indicated here as (a-b). In the language with final devoicing, tableau (1-2), candidate (a) wins over candidate (b) since it satisfies high-ranked markedness. In a language with no final devoicing, on the other hand, tableau (1-3), candidate (b) is the winner. It does not change voicing specification and so satisfies high-ranked IDENT(voice).

Let us now move to forms with a voiceless obstruent word-finally in both languages. Those are the bottom tableaux, indicated here as (c-d). In each case, it is the form with a voiceless obstruent word-finally, candidate (c), that wins. In consequence, in the language with final devoicing, there is neutralization of the voicing distinction on the surface. Inputs distinct in voicing word-finally, /bu**g**/ and /bu**k**/, map onto the same output. In the language with no final devoicing, on the other hand, the underlying voicing distinction is preserved on the surface.

This book considers evidence from a number of languages that shows that a different model of contrast is needed. Based on this evidence, it develops a model of contrast where contrast is stated as an imperative in a phonological system and shows that this model makes different and arguably superior predictions to previous approaches. The core argument rests on the analysis of robust phonological phenomena that involve *contrast transformation*, whereby a given underlying contrast is preserved in the output but manifested as a different surface contrast. In other words, the output manifestation of a given contrast is different from the underlying form.

A well-known example of contrast transformation comes from some dialects of American English where the obstruent voicing contrast as in ri[d]er vs. wri[t]er cannot be manifested by voicing of the vocal cords due to intervocalic flapping but is maintained and realized by lengthening of the preceding vowel, r[a:yɾ]er vs. wr[ayɾ]er, respectively (Fisher and Hirsh 1976) (see (1-4a)).[2] Similarly, in Polish the voicing contrast as in ro[g]i vs. ro[k]i cannot be retained as such in word-final position due to final devoicing. Instead, it is preserved in the output and manifested by the height of the preceding vowel, r[u]k vs. r[o]k, respectively (Gussmann 1980, Rubach 1984) (see (1-4b)).[3] Finally, in Friulian (Hualde 1990, Repetti 1992, 1994, 2000) the voicing contrast as in la[d]e vs. la[t]e cannot be retained in syllable final position due to final devoicing but is preserved and manifested by the length of the preceding vowel l[a:]t vs. l[a]t, respectively (see (1-4c)). The different transformations of the voicing contrast are represented below.

(1-4) Transformations of the voicing contrast

a. Intervocalic flapping in American English (Fisher and Hirsh 1976)

ri[d]er vs. wri[t]er	→	r[a:yɾ]er vs. wr[ayɾ]er 'rider' vs. 'writer'

b. Vowel raising in Polish (Gussmann 1980, Rubach 1984)

ro[g]i vs. ro[k]i	→	r[u]k vs. r[o]k 'horn' vs. 'year'

c. Vowel lengthening in Friulian (Hualde 1990, Repetti 1992, 1994, 2000)

la[d]e vs. la[t]e	→	l[a:]t vs. l[a]t 'gone' (m.) vs. 'milk'

Contrast transformation is not limited to the voicing contrast. It has been recognized that other contrasts can also be manifested on the surface in a different way than in the underlying form (see Donegan and Stampe 1979, Gussmann 1976, Kaye 1974, 1975, Kisseberth 1976, and Łubowicz 2003 among others).

Contrast transformation is not admitted under the simple interaction of markedness and faithfulness constraints in standard OT because the form with contrast transformation incurs a seemingly unmotivated violation of faithfulness. This is illustrated below using the example of English flapping.

(1-5) /ray**d**ər/ → [**ra:y**ɾər] 'rider' – wrong result

/ ray**d**ər/	FLAPPING	IDENT(flap)	IDENT(length)
a. ☞ **ra:y**ɾər		*	!*!
b. ☜ **ray**ɾər		*	

(1-6) /ray**t**ər/ → [**ray**ɾər] 'writer'

/ray**t**ər/	FLAPPING	IDENT(flap)	IDENT(length)
a. ☞ **ray**ɾər		*	
b. **ra:y**ɾər		*	*!

In the above examples, the underlying contrast in obstruent voicing, /ray**d**ər/ vs. /ray**t**ər/, is transformed into the surface contrast in the length of the preceding vowel, [**ra:y**ɾər] vs. [**ray**ɾər], respectively. Standard OT does not admit the form with contrast transformation (see (1-5)). The actual output form in (1-5(a)) incurs a seemingly unmotivated additional violation of faithfulness and thus is ruled out under the simple interaction of markedness and standard faithfulness constraints. Yet, contrast transformation is common cross-linguistically and we need to be able to account for it formally.

Various non-contrast mechanisms have been proposed to account for contrast transformation. Those include rule ordering in rule-based phonology (Kenstowicz and Kisseberth 1979, Kiparsky 1973, Rubach 1984), underspecification (Kiparsky 1993), and more recent proposals such as output–output correspondence (Benua 1997), the Lexical Phonology Model of OT (LPM-OT) (Kiparsky 2000), sympathy theory (McCarthy 1999, 2003a), candidate chains (McCarthy 2007), turbidity (Goldrick and Smolensky 1999), comparative markedness (McCarthy 2003b), and local conjunction (Smolensky 1993), among others. For a discussion of these approaches, see McCarthy (2007). None of these proposals directly refer to contrast or recognize contrast transformation as a property of opaque processes, and none offer a uniform analysis of opaque and transparent processes without additional modifications.

The key idea in this book is that contrast transformation or trading of oppositions is a property of the synchronic grammar and needs to be accounted for by the adopted model of the grammar. A broad range of phenomena from phonology and the phonology-morphology interface that involve contrast transformation will be examined in the following chapters. To account for contrast transformation this book will develop a model of contrast where contrast preservation is stated as an imperative in a phonological system.

1.3 Outline of the book

PC theory is developed in this book as follows: Chapter 2 introduces the theory of contrast called PC theory, while looking at the example of chain shift mappings. The key observation is that chain shifts involve contrast transformation, where a given underlying contrast is preserved in the output but manifested as a different surface contrast. PC theory provides a framework to capture this observation formally. PC theory makes different and arguably superior predictions to previous approaches. Unlike previous approaches, it admits push shift mappings, where the second mapping in the shift is due to contrast and not markedness. PC theory also provides a uniform analysis of transparent and opaque phonological processes, such as chain shifts.

Chapter 3 applies the proposal to the study of phonological contrast using the example of stress-epenthesis interaction in Arabic dialects. The central claim is that in Arabic the underlying contrast in presence versus absence of the vowel is manifested as a surface contrast in stress. It discusses predictions of the model for the typology of stress-epenthesis interaction in Arabic and compares it to previous approaches. Unlike previous approaches, PC theory gives a uniform analysis of contrast-preserving, contrast-neutralizing, and hybrid dialects. It also correctly predicts that onset dialects will always be contrast neutralizing. This chapter also discusses the role of locality in contrast transformation.

Chapter 4 extends the proposal to the study of morphological contrast by examining opaque allomorphy in Polish. One key observation is that in Polish locative, palatalization is non-neutralizing. The underlying contrast in palatalization is manifested as surface contrast in the choice of the allomorph. This provides an account of opaque allomorphy in terms of contrast. Previous accounts of allomorphy are also discussed. The main implication is that PC theory, unlike previous approaches, predicts that there will be cases where allomorphy takes place to preserve contrast.

Finally, Chapter 5 summarizes the results of this book. It further revisits the architecture of PC theory and its implications.

This book is intended for readers who already know the basics of Optimality Theory (OT). Readers who are not familiar with OT are advised to begin with an introduction to OT such as Kager (1999b) or McCarthy (2004) before reading this book. As for how to read this book, I would advise starting with Chapter 2 where the basic elements of PC theory are introduced. Chapters 3 and 4 both build on what is introduced in Chapter 2. Chapters 3 and 4 are fairly independent from one another and can be read in either order. Readers who prefer just a short introduction to PC theory may want to read only section 2.2 which introduces the majority of tools and mechanisms of PC theory.

Notes

1. The words also differ phonetically in the length of the preceding vowel. For more discussion, see Kingston and Diehl (1994).

2. This will be referred to as *contrast displacement* in the phonological grammar where the original contrast between voiced and voiceless obstruents is manifested on the surface in a neutralizing context by the "derived" length of the preceding vowel. The vowels also differ in length in a non-neutralizing context in a more phonetic part of the grammar, called *contrast enhancement*.
3. The process of vowel raising is morphologically restricted in Polish (Gussmann 1980).

2 The framework: PC theory

This chapter develops a formal theory of contrast, called PC theory (for "preserve contrast"). The proposal is introduced by looking at simple cases of neutralization and preservation, and further applied to chain shift mappings. The key observation is that chain shifts involve contrast transformation where a given underlying contrast is traded for another surface contrast. To account for contrast transformation, PC theory proposes that contrast exists as a primitive in a phonological system formulated as a family of rankable and violable constraints. The predictions of PC theory are discussed and compared with alternatives. One of the core implications is that, unlike previous approaches, PC theory admits push shift mappings.

2.1 Statement of the problem

In a phonological chain shift, underlying /A/ maps onto surface [B] and underlying /B/ maps onto surface [C] but, crucially, underlying /A/ does not become surface [C]. Thus, there is a chain shift effect which has a standard representation of: A→B→C (see Dinnsen and Barlow 1998, Gnanadesikan 1997, Kenstowicz and Kisseberth 1979, Kirchner 1996, Labov 1994, McCarthy 1999, Moreton and Smolensky 2002, Parkinson 1996, and Ultan 1970, among others). Finnish vowel shift (Anttila 1995, 2000, 2002, Harrikari 1999, 2000, Karlsson 1999, Keyser and Kiparsky 1984, Lehtinen 1967, McCawley 1964) provides an example.

In Finnish, before the plural suffix -i (similarly before the past tense marker -i), long low vowels shorten (/aa/→[a]), short low vowels undergo rounding (and raising) (/a/→[o]), and short round vowels surface unchanged (/o/→[o]). Thus, we have the following chain shift effect. In the diagram below, arrows indicate input–output mappings.

(2-1) Finnish chain shift

aa → a → o ↻

Some examples are given in (2-2).

(2-2) Examples of Finnish chain shift

	singular nominative		**plural essive**
/aa/→[a]	m**aa**	'earth'	m**a**-i-na
	vap**aa**	'free'	vap**a**-i-na
/a/→[o]	kiss**a**	'cat'	kiss**o**-i-na
	vap**a**	'fishing rod'	vap**o**-i-na
/o/→[o]	tal**o**	'house'	tal**o**-i-na
	pelk**o**	'fear'	pelk**o**-i-na

The key issue is that in Finnish forms with underlying long low vowels shorten but do not round (/aa/→[a],*[o]), but forms with underlying short low vowels undergo rounding in the same context (/a/→[o]).

Chain shifts present a challenge to Optimality Theory (hereafter OT) (Prince and Smolensky 1993/2004) in its original form. OT is *output-oriented*: phonological processes like /aai/→[ai] and /ai/→[oi] bring output forms into conformity with high-ranking markedness constraints. The existence of these processes in Finnish indicates that two markedness constraints, informally *aai and *ai, dominate antagonistic faithfulness constraints. But with both markedness constraints high-ranked, we expect underlying /aai/ to go all the way to [oi], thereby satisfying both markedness constraints. The expected but incorrect mapping is illustrated in (2-3).

(2-3) Expected mapping (cf. (2-1))

aa a → o

Even though chain shifts are problematic for classic OT, they are part of a synchronic mechanism of the grammar and we need to be able to account for them formally. Some examples of vowel height chain shifts come from Basaá (Bantu, Schmidt 1996), Gbanu (Niger-Congo, Bradshaw 1996), Kikuria (Bantu, Chacha and Odden 1994), Lena Spanish (Hualde 1989), Nzɛbi (Clements 1991), and Servigliano Italian (Kaze 1989). These are mostly raising mappings (Parkinson 1996). Some examples of consonantal chain shifts come from Southern Paiute (McLaughlin 1984, Sapir 1930), Toba Batak (Hayes 1986), Estonian (Ultan 1970), Finnish (Ultan 1970), and Irish (Ní Chiosáin 1991). These are mostly lenition mappings on either voicing or consonantal stricture scale (Gnanadesikan 1997). See (2-4) and (2-5), respectively.

(2-4) Vowel shifts (Clements 1991, Labov 1994)

a. New Zealand (Labov 1994): æ → e → i → ɨ
b. Nzɛbi (Bantu: Clements 1991): a → ɛ → e → i , ɔ → o → u

(2-5) Consonantal shifts (Ultan 1970)

a. Southern Paiute (Uto-Aztecan, Sapir 1930): pp → p → v
b. Toba Batak (Austronesian, Hayes 1986): np → pp → ʔp

According to Gnanadesikan (1997) and Kirchner (1996), the solution to chain shift mappings in OT lies in an enriched theory of faithfulness. Both researchers propose special types of faithfulness constraints that block two-step movements like /aai/→[oi], thereby accounting for the discrepancy in phonological mappings between identical derived and underlying segments. Kirchner uses locally conjoined faithfulness constraints, whereas Gnanadesikan distinguishes between classical IDENT-type constraints and novel IDENT-ADJACENT-type constraints on some scale of similarity.[1]

In this book, I will explore an alternative explanation for chain shifts that has implications well beyond this phenomenon. The explanation starts from the observation that chain shifts always preserve one underlying contrast at the expense of neutralizing another underlying contrast. In Finnish, the contrast between underlying /aai/ and /ai/, originally one of length, is preserved, albeit in a different form – as a rounding contrast (underlying /aai/ vs. /ai/ surface [ai] vs. [oi]). The contrast between underlying /ai/ and /oi/, the original rounding contrast, is lost (both become [oi]). Thus:

(2-6)	**Input**		**Output**
	length contrast	→	rounding contrast
	rounding contrast	→	neutralized

Preservation of one contrast taking precedence over preservation of another contrast will be referred to as *contrast transformation.*

As discussed in the introduction (Chapter 1), the main question in this work is where contrast preservation fits into the grammar: whether it follows from other components of the grammar or exists as a primitive. In generative phonology, contrast preservation is an epiphenomenon of rule application. Whether contrasts are preserved or neutralized follows from what rules there are and how they apply in a given language. In standard OT, contrast preservation is also a derivative. It follows from the interaction of markedness and faithfulness constraints that do not themselves refer to contrast. The proposal here is different from both generative phonology and standard OT. It is proposed that contrast preservation exists as an independent principle in the grammar, which in the framework of OT is formulated as a family of rankable and violable constraints on preserving contrasts. I will refer to this proposal as PC theory.

There is a large body of work on the status of contrast in phonology (see references in Chapter 1). This chapter investigates contrast in chain shift mappings.

The next section (section 2.2) presents the elements of the proposal. Section 2.3 illustrates the proposal with a simple case of neutralization and the lack thereof. Section 2.4 shows how the proposal can be applied to analyze Finnish and other chain shifts. Section 2.5 gives the factorial typology. Section 2.6 discusses predictions of the proposal and compares them with previous approaches. Section 2.7 describes the Dispersion Theory of Contrast.

2.2 PC theory

To account for phonological mappings that involve contrast transformation such as chain shifts, I will propose a modification of OT, called PC theory. In PC theory contrast preservation is not just a phenomenon but a formal property of the grammar (cf. Flemming 1995, 1996, Padgett 1997, 2000). It is formalized as competing constraints on preserving contrasts.

PC theory makes a novel prediction as to what can force or block a phonological process. In PC theory phonological mappings are evaluated together, and thus one mapping can force or block another mapping in the same system for reasons of contrast. This prediction is different from other approaches to phonology, where mappings are evaluated in isolation. In the previous approaches, mappings cannot directly activate or block one another. I will illustrate the predictions of PC theory using the example of the Finnish chain shift.[2]

By formulating contrast preservation as an imperative in a phonological system, PC theory provides an explanation for opaque processes (e.g. chain shifts) and explains transparent and opaque phonological processes in a uniform manner with no additional mechanisms required. This is different from previous OT approaches to chain shifts (see section 2.6).

The next section (2.2.1) shows how to form a candidate in PC theory, and the following section (2.2.2) describes the constraints.

2.2.1 A scenario

The central claim of PC theory is that there exist anti-neutralization Preserve Contrast constraints. Constraints on contrast preservation can only be formalized under the assumption that no /input/→[output] mapping takes place in isolation; all such mappings are part of a system (cf. Flemming 1995, Padgett 1997). The key idea is that phonological mappings are not evaluated in isolation but in the context of other mappings in the same system. This is different from standard OT, where mappings are evaluated in isolation. In OT, similar ideas are also present in models of output–output faithfulness (Benua 1997, Gouskova 2004, Kenstowicz 1996) and in the allomorphic model of Burzio (1998).

Formally, in the OT framework this must mean that candidates are sets of mappings, which I will call *scenarios*. The main idea is that mappings influence one another. A mapping can block or force another mapping in a system. The claim is that chain shifts can be understood as part of a system of mappings (a scenario).

To illustrate, let us look at the chain-shift scenario in Finnish. In Finnish, the logic behind a scenario is as follows: underlying /aa/ undergoes shortening before –i and maps onto [a]. This forces underlying /a/ in the same context to move away – it undergoes rounding and maps onto [o]. By rounding, the low vowels distinct in length, /aa/ and /a/, do not neutralize on the surface. They map onto distinct outputs. This has consequences for the system of mappings. The length merger is avoided, but there is another merger that takes place as a consequence. Due to rounding, there is a merger between underlying /a/ and /o/. They both map onto [o]. It is important that the mappings all take place in the same context.

There is another mapping in Finnish that also maps onto [o] and thus is part of the scenario. This is the mapping for underlying /oo/. In Finnish, underlying /oo/ before /i/ shortens with no change in height (/oo/→[o]) and thus merges with the short vowels /a/ and /o/. Some examples of the mapping for underlying /oo/ are given below.

(2-7) Shortening of /oo/

eht**oo**	'evening'	eht**o**-i-na
tien**oo**	'area'	tien**o**-i-na

Altogether, the four mappings constitute part of the chain-shift scenario in Finnish: /aai/→[ai], /ai/→[oi], /oi/→[oi], and /ooi/→[oi]. This is shown below.

(2-8) The chain-shift scenario

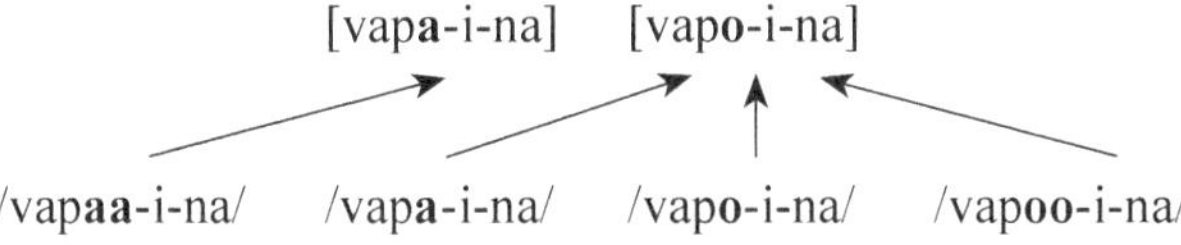

The actual chain-shift scenario competes with other scenarios in the same candidate set. In PC theory, each scenario is a candidate, and rankable constraints determine which scenario is optimal. Some examples of scenarios in a candidate set are given below. Scenarios represent various mapping coexistence patterns.

(2-9) Some scenarios in a candidate set

(i) Identity scenario (Identity map)	(ii) Transparent scenario (Shortening)	(iii) Chain-shift scenario (Shortening and rounding)
[aai] [ai] [ooi] [oi] ↑ ↑ ↑ ↑ /aai/ /ai/ /ooi/ /oi/	[ai] [oi] ↗↑ ↗↑ /aai/ /ai/ /ooi/ /oi/	[ai] [oi] ↗ ↗↗↑ /aai/ /ai/ /ooi/ /oi/

In the identity scenario, each input maps onto an identical output. In the transparent scenario, there is shortening but no rounding. In the actual scenario, there is both shortening and rounding, but rounding targets only underlying short vowels. (In (2-9), I show interacting processes only. As will be explained below, each scenario contains a whole space of mappings.)

In the rest of this section I describe how to formally determine the set of inputs and outputs of a scenario.

The input. "Scenario-inputs" are returned by the function (the operator) *Gen* (cf. Prince and Smolensky 1993/2004). The construction of scenario-inputs is analogous to the role of Gen in Correspondence Theory (McCarthy and Prince 1995). Formally, for a given underlying form Gen returns scenario-inputs. Those are the inputs of each scenario in a candidate set. This is defined below.

(2-10) The role of Gen in PC
Gen (underlying form$_i$) → scenario-inputs$_i$

Gen takes an underlying form as its argument and returns a set of inputs as its value. The set of inputs returned by Gen (scenario-inputs) contains forms (string of segments) that can potentially interact.[3]

The input to Gen is a string of segments (a word) and the outputs are strings that are different from the input in zero or more P (phonological) properties. The P properties are distinctive phonological properties, such as *voicing*, *place*, *manner*, *length*, and so on. Let us put aside length differences for the moment and consider distinctive features other than segmental deletion and insertion. With that in mind, the set of scenario-inputs returned by Gen for a given underlying form contains strings that consist of any sounds (bundles of P properties) and sound combinations that are logically possible.

(2-11) The role of Gen
Gen (underlying form$_i$) → the set of scenario-inputs *i* such that ∀P properties, ∀linear combinations of P, ∃y such that y∈ scenario-inputs$_i$

For example, the set of scenario-inputs for a three-segment underlying form *bad* contains *bad*, *bat*, *pat*, *ugh*, *kl̥o*, and so on. This is illustrated below:

(2-12) Inputs by feature changes
Gen (bad) → {bad, bat, pat, ugh, kl̥o etc.}

In addition to featural differences, the input set also contains forms that differ from the underlying form in the number of segments. Those are forms that contain fewer segments than the underlying form (by deletion), including a null set, and forms that contain more segments (by epenthesis). Some examples for *bad* are *ba*, *a*, *bada*, and so on.

(2-13) Inputs by deletion and insertion
Gen (bad) → {ba, a, bada, etc.}

The way in which scenarios are evaluated, as will be discussed in the next section, demands that scenarios be finite. To prevent unbounded insertion of segments, it will be assumed that there is a limit on the number of segments that can be added to the underlying form. For convenience, there can be only as many segments added to the underlying form as there are original segments plus 1. Formally, epenthesis takes place such that there are two spots adjacent to each segment in a string of segments available for the epenthetic filler. For example, for the input *bad* there are four possible sites of epenthesis, as in: _b_a_d_.[4]

In addition to forms with featural changes (see (2-12)) and deletion or insertion of segments (see (2-13)), there are forms where Gen changes more than one P property in one and the same form. For example, it combines a change in a P property, such as place or manner, with deletion or insertion of segments. Thus, altogether, the set of scenario-inputs returned by Gen for a three-segment underlying form *bad* contains, among other forms, *ba, a, ugh, ug*, and so on.

(2-14) Altogether
Gen (bad) → {ba, a, bada, ugh, ug, pata, etc.}

As a final comment on Gen, I would like to point out that Gen is a universal function, the same for all underlying forms, but scenario-inputs generated by Gen are not universal. The same scenario-inputs are generated for all underlying forms of a given length, length n, but different for underlying forms of different length. Given an underlying form of length n, scenario-inputs generated by Gen are any strings 0…2n+1. The idea is that Gen generates all inputs that could possibly interact. Thus, the same scenario-inputs will be generated for *bad* as for *pat* or *ugh*. This set is different from the one for *pata*, a four-segment underlying form, though there is an overlap between the two scenario-inputs due to deletion and insertion of segments.

It is helpful to think of inputs as distributed in a multi-dimensional space. Inputs generated by Gen form a network, the dimensions of which are determined by the P properties. Here is a subset of the input network defined by three distinct P properties: (a) obstruent voicing in word-final position (x axis), (b) vowel length (y axis), and (c) nasality in word-initial position (z axis).

(2-15) The input network

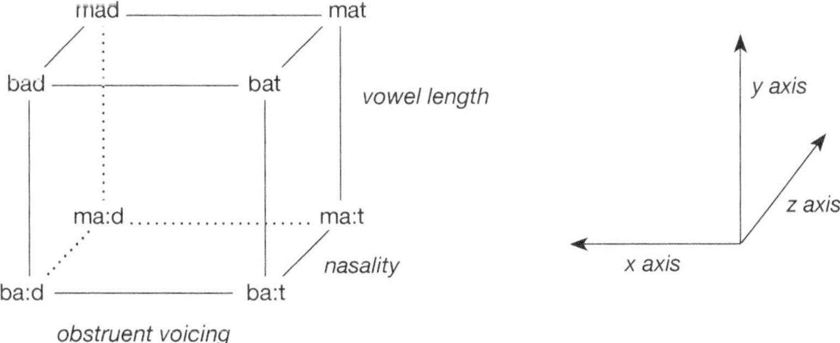

The various P properties define the space of inputs in a scenario. Since a scenario contains a set of input–output mappings, it is also necessary to define what outputs are included in the scenario.

The output. I propose that output scenarios are a mapping of the input set onto itself. Outputs in a scenario are a subset (whether proper or improper) of the input. There is nothing in the output of a scenario that is not also in the input. This limits the space of mappings that are evaluated. We do not go outside the set of forms that constitute scenario-inputs. Consider part of the Finnish scenario that consists of inputs minimally distinct in vowel length and vowel rounding. As shown here, outputs are drawn from the set of inputs.

(2-16) The Finnish scenario

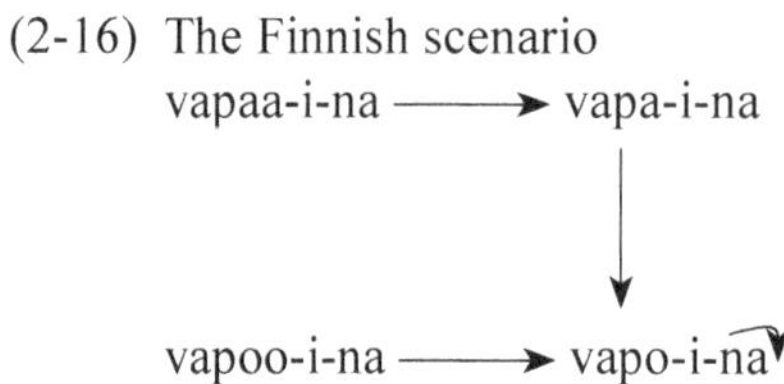

Scenarios represent alternatives that compete for the status of the optimal scenario. Let us look at what scenarios compete with one another in a candidate set.

Scenarios as candidates. Scenarios in a candidate set represent all mappings of the input set into itself. Thus, scenarios in a candidate set have the same inputs but differ in the set of outputs and/or input–output relations even if outputs are the same. As shown in (2-9), the identity scenario has a different set of outputs from the transparent and chain-shift scenarios. The transparent and chain-shift scenarios have the same outputs but differ on the input–output relations. Thus, there are two ways in which scenarios in a candidate set differ from each other: the set of outputs and/or input–output mappings.

The size. Since each scenario represents one of the ways of mapping all the inputs contrasting in some feature(s) onto a subset of itself (whether proper or improper), the size of a scenario is determined by the input. Scenarios in a candidate set are of the same size. They contain the same number of inputs and thus the same number of input–output mappings. Since there is a finite number of oppositions and there is a limit on the length of words in a scenario, a scenario is finite. This is a crucial point if contrast is to be evaluated.

In a tableau, not all of the relevant inputs will be shown. The inputs that will be shown in a tableau will consist of minimally distinct words (words that are distinct on a single P property in one and the same location), that is, *bad* vs. *bat* are minimally distinct but not ***bad*** vs. ***sat***. However, ***bad*** vs. ***sat*** will be included in the scenario in a tableau if their minimally distinct counterparts, ***bat*** and ***sad***, are also included. That is, for any form included in a tableau, there must be a form that is minimally contrastive on some property. Contrasts cross-classify.

Given the way the set of inputs is generated, not all of those forms in the scenario will be the actual words of the language. This is what distinguishes PC theory from accounts where contrast preservation is strictly limited to avoidance of homophony, such as Alderete (2001a, 2001b), Casenhiser (2005), Crosswhite (1997/1999), Ingram (1974), Kisseberth and Abasheikh (1974), Leinonen-Davies (1988), Steriade (1997), and Yip (1988). As discussed in McCarthy (2004) and Albright (2003), homophony avoidance does play a role in synchronic grammar but seems to be limited to paradigmatic relations in derivational morphology. The approach here is similar to the Dispersion Theory of Contrast (Flemming 1995, 2004, Padgett 1997, 2003) because it evaluates contrast among possible words.[5] The claim that a linguistic analysis pertains to possible words of the language and not the existing words is true of both "standard" OT and rule-based treatments, and is not an innovation of PC theory.

The optimal scenario is chosen by the interaction among rankable and violable constraints. These are presented in the next section.

2.2.2 The constraints

As defined in the previous section, a scenario is a space of mappings, with its dimensionality given by contrasting features. Outputs in the scenario are a subset of its inputs. Thus mappings are from the set of inputs onto its subset. (Mappings are output $\subseteq$ input.) Scenarios in a candidate set compete for the status of the optimum. There are three aspects of scenario evaluation: contrast preservation (2.2.2.1), output well-formedness (2.2.2.2), and the degree of input–output disparity in a scenario (2.2.2.3).

Contrast preservation compares scenarios for what types of contrasts are preserved or neutralized in surface forms, and at what costs. There are three aspects of contrast preservation that are evaluated: (i) the number of inputs involved in neutralizations, (ii) the number of outputs that are ambiguous as a result of neutralization, and (iii) the correspondence between input contrasts and output contrasts. Different aspects of contrast preservation take precedence in different languages, and thus different scenarios are optimal in those languages (section 2.2.2.1). In addition, there are constraints on contrast that ensure that contrast is preserved locally (see Chapter 3).

In addition to contrast preservation, scenarios are compared for output well-formedness. Different scenarios may contain different outputs. In addition, since mappings are evaluated together, the same output may correspond to a different number of inputs in different scenarios. That is, scenarios differ not only in the types of outputs but also in the number of particular output forms. Both aspects of output well-formedness are evaluated (section 2.2.2.2).

Finally, different scenarios may fare the same on contrast preservation and output well-formedness but they may differ in the degree of input–output disparity. The same interplay of contrasts and the same output forms can be achieved at various cost. The scenario with the smallest degree of disparity wins. Disparity is evaluated separately for different types of outputs in a scenario (section 2.2.2.3).

The natural set of conditions on mappings in a scenario is summarized below. Recall that these are conditions on contrast preservation, output well-formedness, and input–output disparity, respectively. The condition on contrast preservation has several aspects to it, as mentioned above.

(2-17) Conditions on mappings
- (i) Contrasts are preserved.
  - a. Inputs do not merge.
  - b. Outputs are not ambiguous.

c. Input–output contrasts do not undergo absolute neutralization.
d. Contrast is preserved locally.
(ii) Outputs are well-formed.
(iii) Outputs and corresponding inputs are expressed in the same way.

As will become clear from the following discussion, each of these conditions is indispensable for an effective comparison between scenarios in a candidate set.

In PC theory, each condition is formalized as a family of violable and rankable constraints. These are preserve contrast (PC) constraints, tokenized markedness, and generalized faithfulness. The latter is such that it does not distinguish between different types of identity. The following is a summary of the constraints.

(2-18) Constraints in PC (cf. (2-17))
(i) Preserve contrast (PC)
a. Input-oriented PC
b. Output-oriented PC
c. Relational PC
d. Domain PC
(ii) Tokenized markedness
(iii) Generalized faithfulness/recoverability

Constraints in PC theory belong to two stages of Eval. *Eval* is the evaluator function H that consists of the language-particular constraint hierarchy. In standard OT, Eval is a one-stage constraint ranking. In PC theory, it is proposed that there are two stages of Eval. PC and markedness constraints belong to stage 1 (H-$eval_1$), and generalized faithfulness to stage 2 (H-$eval_2$). This is to avoid redundancy between PC and generalized faithfulness. For example, both PC and generalized faithfulness can block a phonological process. Since Eval is subdivided into two stages, this means that generalized faithfulness constraints can apply only after PC and markedness get a chance to apply. As a result, generalized faithfulness constraints deal with differences between scenarios that have not been determined in H-$eval_1$ by PC or markedness. The two stages of Eval are illustrated below.

(2-19) Structure of PC grammar[6]
a. Gen (underlying $form_i$) → {$Scen_1$, $Scen_2$ …, $Scen_n$}
b. H-$eval_2$ (H-$eval_1$ ($Scen_i$, $1 \leq i < \infty$)) → $Scen_{real}$

Where: H-$eval_1$ = PC and Tokenized markedness
H-$eval_2$ = Generalized faithfulness

Scenarios are first evaluated by PC and markedness in H-$eval_1$. The output of this evaluation process becomes an argument of H-$eval_2$ that consists of a language-particular ranking of generalized faithfulness constraints.

In the following sections I will discuss each constraint family in turn. I will start out with PC constraints, followed by tokenized markedness, and generalized faithfulness. I will then show how the constraints can be used to analyze Finnish and other chain shifts.

2.2.2.1 PC constraints

PC constraints evaluate contrast. There exist four families of PRESERVECONTRAST constraints: input-oriented PC, output-oriented PC, relational PC, and domain PC. Those constraints evaluate scenarios for whether and how they preserve underlying contrasts in surface forms. We need all of them because there are distinct forms of complexity that can inhere in different sets of mappings. The following sections describe input-oriented, output-oriented, and relational PC constraints in more detail (domain PC will be discussed in Chapter 3, section 3.6). When introducing the constraints, I always compare two scenarios, one of which is the actual scenario from Finnish, while the other is a competing scenario from the same candidate set. Let us start out with input-oriented PC.

2.2.2.1.1 Input-oriented PC

Input-oriented PRESERVECONTRAST constraints, $PC_{IN}(P)$ for short, demand that pairs of words that contrast underlyingly in a given phonological property P contrast on the surface (not necessarily in P). Such constraints are defined in (2-20).

(2-20) $PC_{IN}(P)$

For each pair of inputs contrasting in P that map onto the same output in a scenario, assign a violation mark. Formally, assign one mark for every pair of inputs, in_a and in_b, if in_a has P and in_b lacks P, $in_a \rightarrow out_k$, and $in_b \rightarrow out_k$. "If inputs are distinct in P, they need to remain distinct in the output (not necessarily in P)."[7]

What it means to contrast in P is defined as follows.

(2-21) Definition of contrast in P

A pair of inputs, in_a and in_b, contrast in P when corresponding segments in those inputs, seg_a and seg_b, are such that seg_a has P and seg_b lacks P.

This constraint is satisfied when forms are different in phonetic form in the output.

P is a potentially contrastive phonological property, such as a distinctive feature, length, stress, or presence vs. absence of a segment. The properties P, then, are essentially the same as the properties governed by faithfulness constraints in standard OT. Indeed, PC(P) constraints are like faithfulness constraints in that they look at two levels of representation. But they are novel in that they evaluate contrasts for pairs of underlying words and corresponding output words instead of evaluating individual input–output mappings.

Input-oriented PC constraints, unlike standard faithfulness, admit contrast transformation. Since contrasts can be expressed by various properties, $PC_{IN}(P)$ constraints are satisfied even when contrasts are expressed on the surface in a different way than in the underlying form. In Finnish, for example, even though words that contrast underlyingly in length contrast on the surface in rounding, the PC_{IN}(long) constraint is satisfied. As will be discussed below, PC_{IN}(P) constraints by themselves do not determine how to preserve particular contrasts. The way in which a given underlying contrast is expressed on the surface is determined by the interaction of input-oriented PC constraints with each other and with other constraints in the theory.

Another role of input-oriented PC constraints is to minimize the number of mergers in a scenario. Given two scenarios that merge the same types of contrast, input-oriented PC constraints prefer a scenario where fewer input pairs are involved in the same type of merger. Compare the chain-shift scenario to a competing total merger scenario. Both merge length and rounding but the total merger scenario merges those properties for more input pairs and thus is non-optimal on input-oriented PC. The two scenarios are shown below.

(2-22)

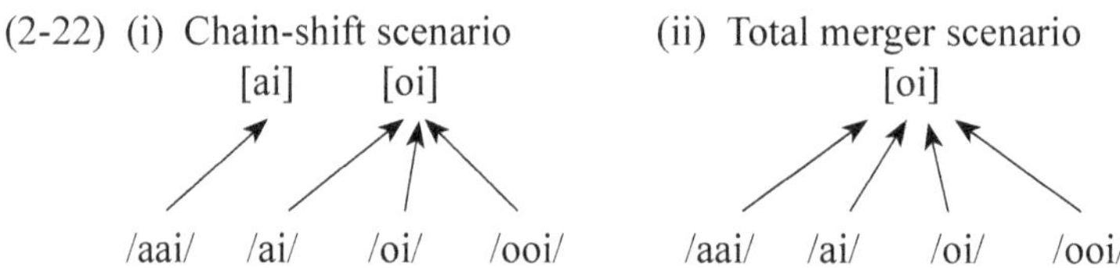

The following table shows violations of input-oriented PC constraints in these scenarios.

(2-23) Constraint violations (unranked)

Scenarios		PC_{IN} (long)	PC_{IN} (round)
(i) Chain shift aai → ai ↓ ooi → oi	/vap**aa**-i-na/ → vap**a**-i-na /vap**a**-i-na/ → vap**o**-i-na /vap**oo**-i-na/ → vap**o**-i-na /vap**o**-i-na/ → vap**o**-i-na	** {/ai/, /ooi/} {/oi/, /ooi/}	** {/ai/, /oi/} {/ai/, /ooi/}
(ii) Total merger aai ai ↘ ↓ ooi → oi	/vap**aa**-i-na/ → vap**o**-i-na /vap**a**-i-na/ → vap**o**-i-na /vap**oo**-i-na/ → vap**o**-i-na /vap**o**-i-na/ → vap**o**-i-na	**** {/ai/, /ooi/} {/oi/, /ooi/} {/ai/, /aai/} {/oi/, /aai/}	**** {/ai/, /oi/} {/ai/, /ooi/} {/aai/, /oi/} {/aai/, /ooi/}

The chain-shift scenario merges two input pairs distinct in length, {/oi/, /ooi/}, {/ai/, /ooi/}. The corresponding total merger scenario, on the other hand, merges four input pairs distinct in length, {/oi/, /ooi/}, {/ai/, /ooi/}, {/ai/, /aai/}, {/oi/, /aai/}. The same goes for rounding. In the chain-shift scenario, there are two input pairs that merge rounding, {/ai/, /oi/}, {/ai/, /ooi/}. In the total merger scenario, rounding is neutralized for four input pairs, {/ai/, /oi/}, {/ai/, /ooi/}, {/aai/, /oi/}, {/aai/, /ooi/}. Thus, the total merger scenario would never win on input-oriented PC constraints over the chain-shift scenario since it incurs more mergers of each type.

2.2.2.1.2 Output-oriented PC

In addition to input mergers, scenarios are evaluated for the ambiguity of their outputs. A scenario with fewer ambiguous outputs is preferred, all else being equal. This is the role of output-oriented PC, $PC_{OUT}(P)$, as defined below.

(2-24) $PC_{OUT}(P)$

For each output that corresponds to two or more inputs contrasting in P assign a violation mark. Formally, assign one mark for every output, out_k, if $in_a \rightarrow out_k$, $in_b \rightarrow out_k$, in_a has P, and in_b lacks P.

"Avoid outputs ambiguous in P property."

The primary role of output-oriented PC is to ensure that if mergers take place in a scenario they are accumulated in one location rather than distributed among outputs. This often forces a merger along some additional dimension of contrast. Compare the chain-shift scenario to a transparent scenario. These are shown below.

(2-25) (i) Chain-shift scenario (ii) Transparent scenario

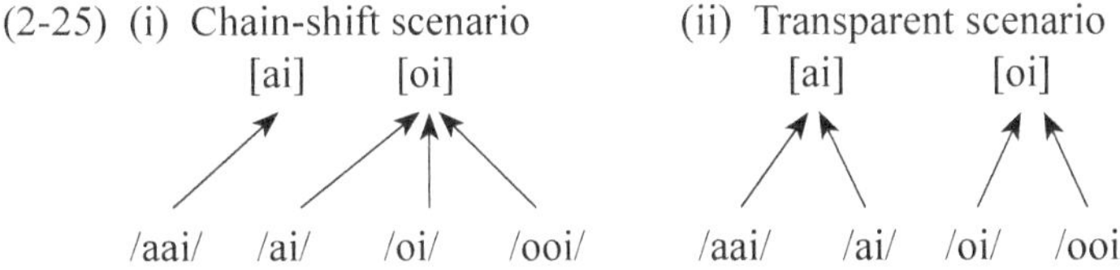

The following table shows violations of output- and input-oriented PC constraints in these scenarios.

(2-26) Constraint violations (unranked)

Scenarios		PC_{OUT} (long)	PC_{IN} (long)	PC_{IN} (round)	PC_{OUT} (round)
(i) Chain shift aai → ai ↓ ooi → oi	/vap**aa**-i-na/ → vap**a**-i-na /vap**a**-i-na/ → vap**o**-i-na /vap**oo**-i-na/ → vap**o**-i-na /vap**o**-i-na/ → vap**o**-i-na	* [oi]	** {/oi/, /ooi/} {/ai/, /ooi/}	** {/ai/, /oi/} {/ai/, /ooi/}	* [oi]
(ii) Transparent aai → ai ooi → oi	/vap**aa**-i-na/ → vap**a**-i-na /vap**a**-i-na/ → vap**a**-i-na /vap**oo**-i-na/ → vap**o**-i-na /vap**o**-i-na/ → vap**o**-i-na	** [ai] [oi]	** {/aai/, /ai/} {/ooi/, /oi/}		

The two scenarios differ in the distribution of length neutralizations among outputs. The chain-shift scenario contains one output ambiguous in length, the [oi] output. The transparent scenario contains two such outputs, [ai] and [oi]. Thus, in the chain-shift scenario there are fewer outputs that correspond to inputs distinct in length. This is at the cost of merging rounding. There are no rounding neutralizations in the transparent scenario but there are some in the chain-shift scenario. In the chain-shift scenario two pairs of inputs merge in rounding: {/ai/,/oi/} and {/ai/,/ooi/}.

As will be shown, in Finnish PC_{OUT}(long) ranked above $PC_{IN/OUT}$(round) selects the chain-shift scenario over the transparent scenario since the chain-shift scenario contains fewer outputs ambiguous in length. When ranked higher than PC constraints against rounding mergers, this constraint forces a merger in rounding. As a result, length neutralizations are accumulated in one location in this scenario rather than distributed among outputs.

When neutralizations cluster, there are fewer outputs in a scenario that are ambiguous in some property P. If the number of ambiguous outputs is taken to be an indication of the recoverability of a scenario, output-oriented PC constraints increase recoverability. For previous work on recoverability see Gussmann (1976), Kaye (1974, 1975), and Kisseberth (1976). See also evidence for clustering of faithfulness violations in the work of Burzio (1996, 1998). Predecessors of output-oriented PC constraints include output-oriented IDENT-type constraints (see Keer 2000, Pater 1999, and Struijke 2001).

2.2.2.1.3 Input- and output-oriented PC

In many cases, input- and output-oriented PC constraints play the same role. They both prohibit neutralizations of particular contrasts. Thus, they are partially overlapping. The difference between the two lies in whether they count neutralizations from the input or the output. This is an important difference when comparing scenarios.

Consider two scenarios with length and rounding mergers, the same number of ambiguous outputs, but a different number of input mergers.

(2-27) (i) Chain-shift scenario (ii) Total merger scenario

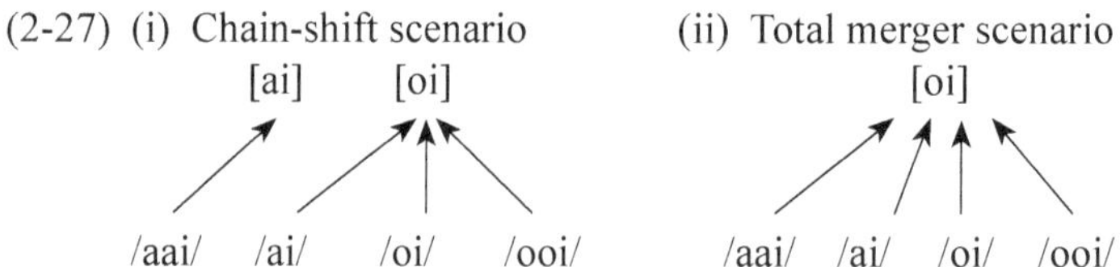

To compare the two scenarios, we need input-oriented PC. Output-oriented PC does not see the difference since it does not count the number of inputs involved in neutralizations. For output-oriented PC, the two scenarios are the same. As will be explained in section 2.5, if there were no input-oriented PC constraints the total merger scenario would always win over the chain-shift scenario (or any other opaque scenario).

Conversely, output-oriented PC is needed to see the virtues of the chain-shift scenario over a transparent scenario.

(2-28) (i) Chain-shift scenario (ii) Transparent scenario

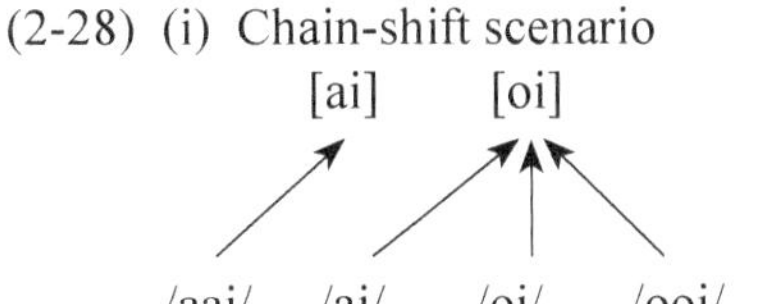

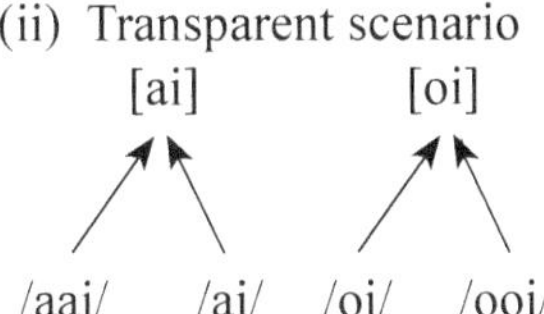

Input-oriented PC would always prefer the transparent scenario since it avoids merging along one additional dimension of contrast. In the transparent scenario, there are only length mergers. In the opaque scenario, there are both length and rounding mergers. In terms of constraints, PC_{IN}(long) constraint is violated twice in both scenarios. PC_{IN}(round) constraint is violated only in the opaque scenario. Thus, the opaque scenario is harmonically bounded by the transparent scenario on input-oriented PC constraints. To ensure that the opaque scenario has a chance to win, we need output-oriented PC constraints. PC_{OUT}(long) prefers the opaque scenario since it reduces the number of outputs ambiguous in length.

The output-oriented PC constraint redistributes neutralizations in a scenario onto one output. As a result, there are fewer outputs ambiguous in some property P.

2.2.2.1.4 Relational PC

In PC theory, there are also relational PC constraints. The logic behind relational PC is as follows: even though in chain shifts (and other opaque processes) some contrast is preserved at the cost of neutralizing some other contrast – in Finnish length is preserved at the cost of neutralizing rounding – there are limits on how many instances of the rounding contrast are neutralized. Too much neutralization may result in an output contrast that does not reflect any minimal instances of an identical input contrast. In Finnish, for example, transforming too many instances of the length contrast into the rounding contrast may result in an output rounding contrast that does not correspond to any instances of the minimal rounding contrast from the input. We can go even further and say that when this happens, the identity of the output contrast is non-recoverable. The output contrast bears no relation to its source. Relational PC militates against it.

Relational PC is related to the Alternation Condition in Kiparsky (1971), which prohibits absolute neutralizations. The Alternation Condition bans positing underlying oppositions that are always neutralized on the surface. The following formulation is given by Kenstowicz and Kisseberth (1979: 215).

(2-29) Alternation Condition

> Each language has an inventory of segments appearing in underlying representations. Call these segments phonemes. The U(nderlying) R(epresentation) of a morpheme may not contain a phoneme /x/ that is always realized phonetically as identical to the realization of some other phoneme /y/.

In short, the Alternation Condition prohibits positing an opposition /x/ vs. /y/ that is always neutralized on the surface.

Similar to the Alternation Condition, relational PC guards identity between output contrasts and their input correspondents. It demands that a given output contrast correspond to at least one instance of an identical minimal input contrast. Relational PC is defined below:

(2-30) $PC_{REL}(P)$

For a pair of outputs minimally contrasting in P that docs not correspond to a pair of inputs minimally contrasting in P, assign a violation mark. Formally, assign one mark for every pair of outputs, out_a and out_b, $|out_a - out_b| = P$, if there is no pair of inputs, in_i and in_j, $\{in_i, in_j\} \rightarrow \{out_a, out_b\}$, and $|in_i - in_j| = P$.
"No absolute neutralization of contrasts."

Relational PC puts limits on contrast permutations. Too much transformation violates relational PC, and thus a conflict results between relational PC and contrast transformation. Given two scenarios that transform contrasts, a scenario in which contrast relation is lost in all instances loses on relational PC. [8]

Compare the chain-shift scenario as in (2-31(i)) to a competing bi-directional scenario (2-31(ii)) (bi-directional since it contains movement going in opposite directions). In both, the length contrast is preserved at the cost of neutralizing rounding. In the chain-shift scenario, the length contrast is preserved for two pairs of inputs and realized as a surface contrast in rounding; both /aai/ vs. /ai/ and /aai/ vs. /oi/ map onto [ai] vs. [oi]. The two other input-length contrasts in this scenario, /ooi/ vs. /oi/ and /ooi/ vs. /ai/, are neutralized. In the bi-directional scenario, on the other hand, length contrast is preserved for every pair of inputs and realized as a surface contrast in rounding, /aai/ vs. /ai/, /ooi/ vs. /oi/, /aai/ vs. /oi/, and /ooi/ vs. /ai/ are all realized as [ai] vs. [oi].

(2-31) (i) Chain-shift scenario

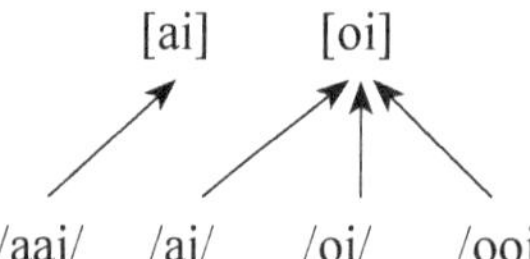

(ii) Bi-directional scenario

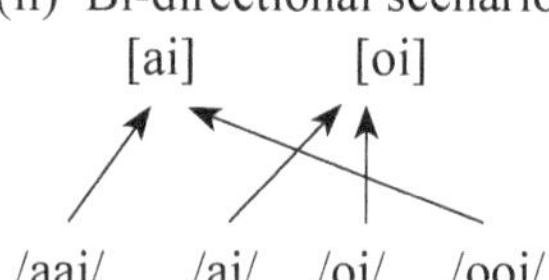

Given the high preference for preserving length contrasts in Finnish, the bi-directional scenario is expected to come out optimal. It preserves every length contrast from the input.

However, as a result of preserving length for each pair of inputs, in the bi-directional scenario each minimal rounding contrast from the input is neutralized: /aai/ vs. /ooi/ and /ai/ vs. /oi/ map onto [ai] and [oi], respectively. A minimal contrast in P refers to pairs that are distinct only by P. As a result, in the bi-directional scenario, the output rounding contrast does not correspond to any of the minimal instances of the rounding contrast from the input. As already mentioned, when this happens, the identity of the output contrast is non-recoverable. This is illustrated in (2-32). The diagram indicates minimal rounding contrasts from the input. Contrasts that are neutralized are indicated with an asterisk.

(2-32) Bi-directional scenario

Non-recoverable identity

[ai] [oi]

/aai/ /ai/ /oi/ /ooi/

*ai~oi

*aai~ooi

In the bi-directional scenario, the identity of the output rounding contrast is non-recoverable since neither /aai/ vs. /ooi/ nor /ai/ vs. /oi/ are preserved. Graphically, both contrasts get an asterisk.

In the chain-shift scenario, on the other hand, the output rounding contrast corresponds to one minimal instance of the rounding contrast from the input. While one of the minimal rounding pairs neutralizes – /ai/ vs. /oi/ both map onto [oi] – the other pair, /aai/ vs. /ooi/, maps onto distinct outputs, [ai] vs. [oi]. Thus, in the chain-shift scenario, unlike in the bi-directional scenario, the identity of the output rounding contrast is recoverable. A minimal rounding contrast from the input, /aai/ vs. /ooi/, is preserved.

(2-33) Chain-shift scenario

Recoverable identity

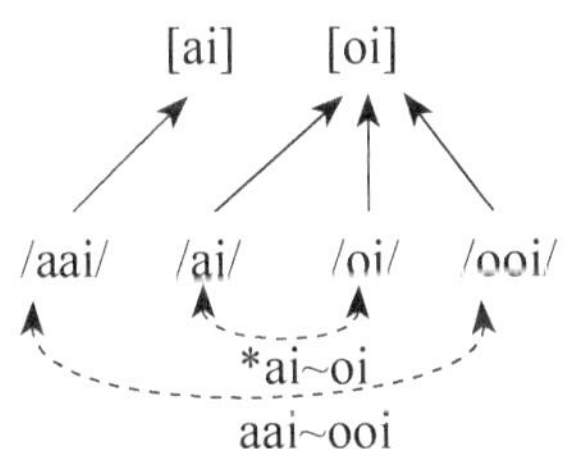

Graphically, only one contrast, /ai/ vs. /oi/, gets an asterisk.

In Finnish, the high-ranking PC_{REL}(round) constraint chooses the chain-shift scenario over the bi-directional scenario, since the chain-shift scenario retains some identity between its output and input rounding contrasts. The choice is made in favor of the chain-shift scenario, even though it is the bi-directional scenario that avoids length mergers altogether. Thus, in Finnish, relational PC is in conflict with PC constraints against length mergers. The choice is made in favor of relational PC.[9]

2.2.2.2 Tokenized markedness

In addition to PC constraints, there are also markedness constraints in the theory. Markedness constraints are indispensable to ignite a shift. As will become apparent, without high-ranking markedness, there would be no movement in a scenario since PC constraints themselves cannot initiate movement (see section 2.6 for discussion). By movement, I mean any unfaithful mapping in a scenario.

In standard OT, markedness constraints evaluate output well-formedness. The same role of markedness is retained in PC theory. In Finnish, for example, high-ranking markedness against tri-moraic syllables accounts for shortening. It is more important to avoid tri-moraic syllables than to preserve length contrasts. But in PC theory the concept of markedness is taken a step further. Scenarios are different not only on output types but also on how many outputs of a particular type there are in a scenario (the number of outputs equals the number of inputs that map onto them). Since markedness in PC theory counts the number of output types, it is called tokenized markedness.

(2-34) TOKENIZED MARKEDNESS
Assign a violation mark for every instance of output, out_x, where the number of outputs equals the number of inputs that map onto out_x.
"Assign a violation mark for every token of a marked output in a scenario, where the number of tokens equals the number of inputs that map onto this output."

When there is no output x in a scenario, tokenized markedness is satisfied. When there is an output x, tokenized markedness is violated and it distinguishes between scenarios with different numbers of inputs that map onto x. Since there are markedness constraints against various types of outputs and they are ranked with respect to one another, tokenized markedness constraints decide which output in a scenario is a preferred site for neutralization. The less marked output is the one that is preferred according to markedness. It is better to have more instances of a less marked output in a scenario than of its more marked competitor.

Consider two competing chain-shift scenarios. The two scenarios have the same set of outputs but differ on which output is the site of neutralization. In the chain-shift scenario (2-35(i)), the output with the [oi] diphthong is the site of neutralization, [vapoina]. In the mirror-image scenario (2-35(ii)), it is the output with the [ai] diphthong, [vapaina]. The scenarios are represented vertically to better illustrate the difference.

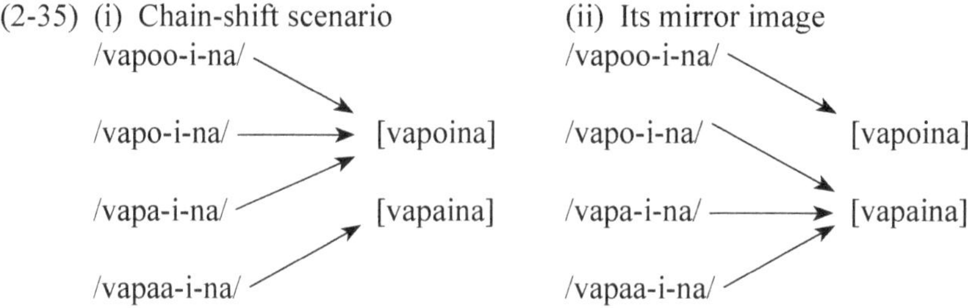

The following table shows violations of tokenized markedness in the two scenarios.

(2-36) Constraint violations (unranked)

Scenarios		*ai	*oi
(i) Chain shift aai → ai ↓ ooi → oi (circular)	/vap**aa**-i-na/ → vap**a**-i-na /vap**a**-i-na/ → vap**o**-i-na /vap**oo**-i-na/ → vap**o**-i-na /vap**o**-i-na/ → vap**o**-i-na	* /aai/ → [ai]	*** /ai/ → [oi] /oi/ → [oi] /ooi/ → [oi]
(ii) Mirror image aai → ai (circular) ↑ ooi → oi	/vap**aa**-i-na/ → vap**a**-i-na /vap**a**-i-na/ → vap**a**-i-na /vap**oo**-i-na/ → vap**o**-i-na /vap**o**-i-na/ → vap**a**-i-na	*** /aai/ → [ai] /ai/ → [ai] /oi/ → [ai]	* /ooi/ → [oi]

Tokenized markedness makes the choice between the two scenarios. The scenario with neutralization onto [vapoina], the chain-shift scenario, creates more outputs of type [oi]. The scenario with neutralization onto [vapaina], the mirror-image scenario, contains more tokens of type [ai]. Depending on the relative ranking of tokenized markedness constraints, *ai versus *oi, one or the other scenario is more harmonic. If [vapoina] is a better output than [vapaina], then the chain-shift scenario is more harmonic. With the opposite ranking, its mirror image wins.

The two scenarios in (2-35) differ in directionality of movement. The chain-shift scenario contains rounding, the competing mirror-image scenario contains lowering. Tokenized markedness makes the choice between the two.

To conclude, tokenized markedness constraints have two roles in the theory: (i) they force movement in a scenario by evaluating output well-formedness, and (ii) they evaluate directionality of movement by counting the number of marked tokens in a scenario. Thus, tokenized markedness constraints combine the notions of standard markedness and faithfulness. They are like standard markedness since they evaluate output well-formedness. But they are also like standard faithfulness since they have access to the input as well as to the output. Consequently, like standard markedness, they can force a phonological process and like standard faithfulness, they can determine directionality of movement in a scenario.[10]

2.2.2.3 Generalized faithfulness

Markedness and PC constraints constitute the core of PC theory. They belong to stage 1 of Eval and perform the initial screening of scenarios in a candidate set. However, they do not make all necessary distinctions between scenarios. Therefore, once markedness and PC get a chance to trim down the candidate set, faithfulness comes into play. In PC faithfulness constraints belong to stage 2 of Eval. Their role is solely to resolve ties from stage 1. As will become apparent, this is a much more reduced version of faithfulness than the one in standard OT. The reduction of faithfulness is expected in the light of the transfer of much of its responsibility to PC constraints and tokenized markedness.

In PC theory faithfulness has two goals: (i) it rules out scenarios that involve unnecessary movement (movement that is not motivated by either PC or markedness), and (ii) it helps determine the directionality of movement in a scenario. Movement in PC theory is understood as any type of input–output disparity for each mapping in a scenario. In the following discussion, I will first describe how faithfulness rules out unnecessary movement and then show how it determines the directionality of movement in a scenario.

Faithfulness constraints in PC theory are not the same as faithfulness constraints in standard OT. Faithfulness constraints in PC sum up violations of identity for all mappings in a scenario and they treat any change – rounding, nasalization, deletion or insertion – the same way. Since they do not distinguish between different types of non-identity, they are called *generalized* faithfulness constraints. This is the main difference between generalized faithfulness and standard faithfulness.

Standard faithfulness distinguishes between different types of non-identity. There are distinct standard faithfulness constraints that militate against a change in rounding, IDENT(round), and different faithfulness constraints that militate against a change in nasality, IDENT(nasal). In PC theory, these are expressed under one and the same constraint. The role of generalized faithfulness, therefore, is to evaluate the cost of achieving a certain interplay of contrasts and markedness in the system. Given a choice between scenarios that fare equally on markedness and PC, generalized faithfulness constraints choose a scenario where inputs and outputs are most similar to each other.

Below I give a preliminary definition of generalized faithfulness. This definition will be modified once the other goal of faithfulness, directionality of movement, has been discussed.

(2-37) GENERALIZED FAITHFULNESS (first pass)
An output is identical to its input correspondent in every property. Assign a violation mark for any type of disparity (e.g. featural change, deletion, insertion).

Consider two scenarios which are alike except for the degree of input–output disparity. The two scenarios are the transparent scenario with shortening (2-38(i)) and multi-directional scenario with shortening, lowering, and rounding (2-38(ii)).

(2-38) (i) Transparent scenario (ii) Multi-directional scenario

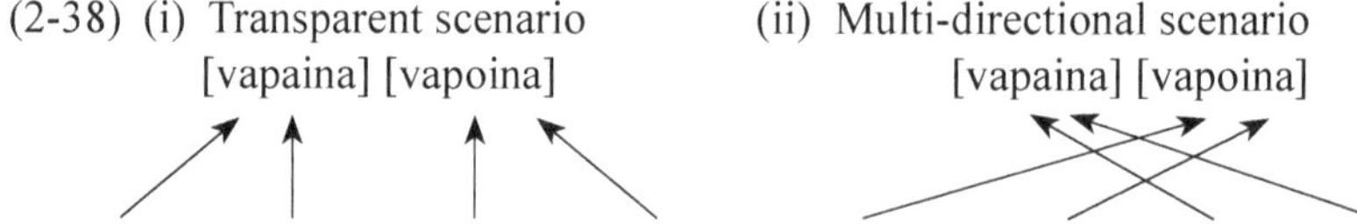

/vapaaina/ /vapaina/ /vapoina/ /vapooina//vapaaina/ /vapaina/ /vapoina/ /vapooina/

The two scenarios fare the same on markedness and PC. They contain the same outputs and the same number of them (tokenized markedness). They merge the same type and number of input pairs (input-oriented PC). They also both contain the same two ambiguous outputs (output-oriented PC). But the two scenarios are different and the theory should be able to express this formally. This is where generalized faithfulness comes into play.

The two scenarios differ in the degree of disparity between inputs and their corresponding outputs. In the multi-directional scenario, outputs and corresponding inputs are more distant than in the competing transparent scenario. Faithfulness rules in favor of the transparent scenario since it contains less movement. In fact, generalized faithfulness harmonically binds the multi-directional scenario. The same is true for so-called permuted scenarios, and circular shift scenarios (see section 2.5).

To distinguish between the transparent and multi-directional scenarios, it would be enough for faithfulness to be formulated as a general constraint against input–output disparity. This constraint would then sum up violations of disparity for each mapping in a scenario. However, as the following example shows, a more detailed formulation of the constraint is needed.

Consider two bi-directional scenarios. They are called bi-directional since they contain both rounding (raising) and lowering.

(2-39) (i) Bi-directional scenario (ii) Its mirror image

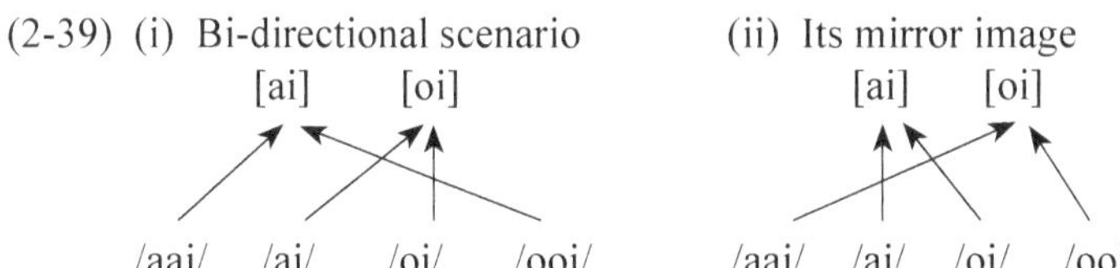

The two scenarios tie on PC and markedness. As far as PC constraints are concerned, both scenarios incur the same types of mergers and involve the same number of inputs and outputs in each merger. As far as markedness goes, both scenarios contain the same outputs and the same number of them. The two scenarios also contain the same degree of input–output disparity since they change length and rounding to the same degree. But the two scenarios are clearly distinct. I will propose that it is the role of generalized faithfulness to distinguish between them.

The two scenarios differ on what the long and short vowels map onto. In (2-39(i)), the long vowels map onto the unrounded vowel output. In (2-39(ii)), the long vowels map onto the rounded vowel output. Since long vowels shorten, the mapping involving long vowels is less faithful than a comparable mapping involving short vowels (/aai/ → [ai] is less faithful than /ai/ → [ai]). Thus, the two scenarios differ in the distribution of unfaithful mappings across outputs. In (2-39(i)), it is the unrounded vowel output that is less faithful. In (2-39(ii)), it is the rounded vowel output.

To capture this observation formally, I propose that in addition to militating against unnecessary input–output disparity, generalized faithfulness constraints evaluate disparity separately for different types of outputs in a scenario (the type of output is determined by the presence/absence of the P property). Since faithfulness is evaluated with respect to the type of output, formally, it takes the output segment as its modifier. One can think of it as partitioning the space of outputs into P sets (divided by the type of output) and then evaluating disparity for each mapping in a set. The constraint is defined below.

(2-40) [αP]-FAITH (cf. (2-37))
An [αP] output is identical to its input correspondent in every property. Assign a violation mark for any type of disparity (e.g. featural change, deletion, insertion).

The key idea is that some sets of P properties tend to be more resistant to unfaithful mappings than others, and thus faithfulness, subcategorized to a set, can determine which types of segment(s) can receive a mapping.

Let us evaluate the two bi-directional scenarios with respect to the constraint defined in (2-40). The two scenarios differ on where long and short vowels map. In (2-39(i)), long vowels map onto [ai], the output with the unrounded vowel. In (2-39(ii)), they map onto [oi], its rounded counterpart. This has consequences for generalized faithfulness. In the scenario where long vowels map onto [ai], (2-39(i)), it is the unrounded vowel [ai] that is less faithful, whereas in the other scenario, (2-39(ii)), it is the rounded counterpart [oi] that fares worse on faithfulness. Depending on the relative ranking of generalized faithfulness constraints, *unrounded*-FAITH versus *rounded*-FAITH, one or the other scenario comes out optimal.[11]

Thus, generalized faithfulness that belongs to stage 2 of Eval has two goals: (i) it minimizes input–output disparity, and (ii) it determines directionality of movement in cases when the choice is not already made on tokenized markedness. (Tokenized markedness which determines directionality of movement in stage 1 of Eval would not be able to distinguish between the two bi-directional scenarios. Both scenarios fare the same on tokenized markedness: they have the same outputs and the same number of them.)

The generalized faithfulness constraint can be seen as a combination of faithfulness and markedness. It is a faithfulness constraint since it evaluates input–output identity but it is also subcategorized to a particular output and in that, resembles standard markedness. The idea behind generalized faithfulness is that some outputs are more faithful than other outputs.[12]

In cases of contrast displacement where input contrast is preserved in the output but realized in a different location than in the input (see Chapters 3 and 4), generalized faithfulness constraints are formulated as recoverability constraints. See the relevant chapters for a definition of the constraint on recoverability.

The next section shows how PC constraints interact with each other, conflicting markedness constraints, and low-ranked faithfulness in choosing the optimal scenario.

2.3 Illustration of the proposal

Here is an example of how the constraints work on a simple case of neutralization and the lack of it.[13]

2.3.1 Neutralization: final devoicing

Consider a language with final devoicing. For final devoicing to take place, markedness against voiced obstruents syllable-finally must outrank conflicting PC. It is more important to avoid voiced obstruents syllable-finally than it is to preserve contrast in voicing. The neutralization ranking is given below.

(2-41) Neutralization ranking
*VOICEDOBSTRUENT]$_\sigma$ >> PC_{IN}(voice), PC_{OUT}(voice)

This is illustrated in the following tableau. Scenarios are formed as described in section 2.2.1. For a given three-segment underlying form, scenario-inputs are all strings of length 0–7. These are all possible combinations of all P (phonological) properties including deletion and insertion of segments. For example, scenario-inputs for underlying form *vad* contain, among others, *vad* (the identity form), *vat* (by final devoicing), *va* (by deletion), *va:* (by deletion and lengthening), *ba* (by deletion and change in place), and *thad* (by change in place). The inputs shown in the tableau are a subset of these. They are minimally distinct in obstruent voicing word-finally, ***vad*** vs. ***vat.*** (This is a standard procedure in OT, where not all forms are shown in a tableau.) In each scenario outputs are a subset (possibly improper) of the inputs. In scenario (i), the set of outputs is a proper subset of the input. In scenarios (ii) and (iii), the set of outputs is identical to the set of inputs. We now come to the evaluation.

(2-42) Final devoicing takes place

Scenarios		*VOI OBS]$_\sigma$	PC_{IN} (voice)	PC_{OUT} (voice)	(+vd)-FAITH	(-vd)-FAITH
(i) Neutralization ☞ (Polish)	/**vad**/ → vat /**vat**/ → vat		* {/vad/, /vat/}	* [vat]		* d→t
(ii) Identity (English)	/**vad**/ → vad /**vat**/ → vat	*!				
(iii) Permuted (Not attested)	/**vad**/ → vat /**vat**/ → vad	*!			* t→d	* d→t

Scenario (i), the neutralization scenario, is the winner as it satisfies high-ranked markedness. It contains no outputs with a voiced obstruent syllable-finally. The other two scenarios, scenario (ii) and scenario (iii), violate high-ranked markedness since they contain a form with a voiced obstruent in a word-final position. The neutralization scenario, scenario (i), incurs some PC violations – it merges contrast for one pair of inputs (violation of input-oriented PC) and in so doing creates an ambiguous output (violation of output-oriented PC), but PC constraints are low-ranked and so are less important than high-ranked markedness. Faithfulness violations are irrelevant here since the choice between candidates is already made in stage 1 of Eval, even before faithfulness gets a chance to apply. There is one violation of faithfulness in the actual scenario since there is voicing disparity in one of the mappings. There are two violations in the permuted scenario, scenario (iii), since there is voicing disparity in both mappings. (The permuted scenario will be discussed in more detail in the following section.)

2.3.2 Lack of neutralization

Now consider the lack of neutralization. In this case, the underlying voicing contrast is preserved on the surface. In terms of a constraint ranking, PC dominates conflicting markedness. It is more important to preserve contrast than to avoid forms that violate markedness. The relevant ranking is below:

(2-43) Lack of neutralization
PC_{IN}(voice), PC_{OUT}(voice) >> *VOICEDOBSTRUENT$]_{\sigma}$

This is illustrated in the following tableau. Scenarios are formed as in the previous case.[14]

(2-44) No devoicing

Scenarios		PC_{IN} (voice)	PC_{OUT} (voice)	*VOI OBS$]_{\sigma}$	(+vd)-FAITH	(-vd)-FAITH
(i) Neutralization (Polish)	/nid/ → nit /nit/ → nit	* {/nid/,/nit/}	*! [nit]			* d→t
(ii) Identity ☞ (English)	/nid/ → nid /nit/ → nit			*		
(iii) Permuted (Not attested)	/nid/ → nit /nit/ → nid			*	* t→d	*! d→t

Here the identity scenario, scenario (ii), is the winner as it satisfies high-ranked PC. In this scenario, forms distinct in voicing are kept distinct even at the cost of violating markedness. The neutralization scenario, scenario (i), loses on PC.

The above tableau also illustrates the role of low-ranked FAITHFULNESS. Consider the so-called permuted scenario, candidate (iii), which is like the identity scenario except that in this scenario outputs correspond to different inputs. The choice between candidate (ii), the identity scenario, and candidate (iii), the permuted scenario, cannot be made on PC or markedness. The two fare the same on those two types of constraints. This is where we need faithfulness. Faithfulness favors candidate (ii) (the identity scenario) over candidate (iii) (the permuted scenario).

In the identity scenario, outputs are closer to their inputs than in the competing permuted scenario (in fact they are the same), and this is preferred, all else being equal.

This illustrates an important prediction of PC theory that is different from rule-based approaches but similar to standard OT. In rule-based approaches mappings take place as long as there exist rules of a particular type. In standard OT, mappings are more restricted. They take place only when they improve on markedness (Moreton 1996/1999). In PC theory, similarly, generalized faithfulness rules out unnecessary movement. For movement to take place, it must improve on either contrast or markedness. Otherwise, it will not take place. (For a discussion of this prediction see section 2.6.)

So far, PC works similarly to standard faithfulness. When markedness dominates conflicting PC, a phonological process takes place. When PC dominates conflicting markedness, a phonological process is blocked. The next section points to differences between PC and standard faithfulness.

2.4 Application to chain shifts

As has been observed, in Finnish the underlying length contrast is preserved despite shortening and realized as surface contrast in rounding. Some instances of the original rounding contrast are neutralized as a result. This is called *contrast transformation.*

Compare the chain-shift scenario to a competing transparent scenario. In both scenarios there is shortening but only the chain-shift scenario involves rounding. In the chain-shift scenario, due to rounding, the length contrast is preserved for one minimal pair of inputs despite shortening. The length contrast is realized as a rounding contrast; /aai/ vs. /ai/ is manifested as [ai] vs. [oi]. In the transparent scenario, on the other hand, there is no rounding, and thus the two inputs, /aai/ vs. /ai/, map onto the same output. In (2-45) below, the relevant input pair is boxed.

(2-45) (i) Chain-shift scenario (ii) Transparent scenario

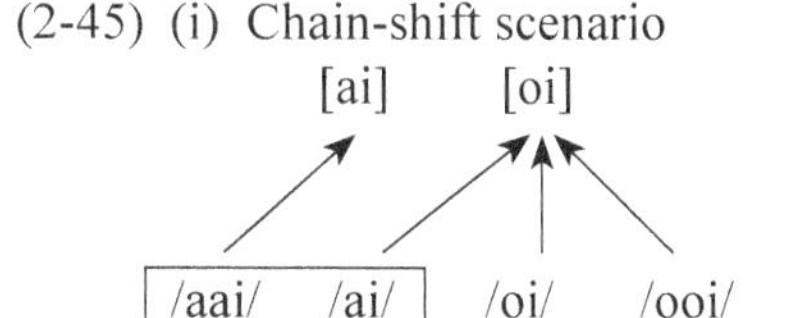

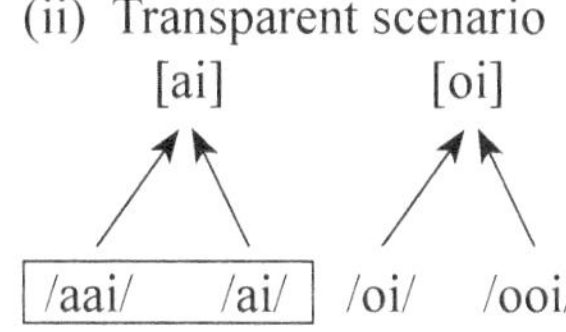

Shortening neutralizes all minimal length contrasts in the transparent scenario but is non-neutralizing for some input contrasts in the chain-shift scenario. Preservation of the length contrast versus its neutralization is the crucial difference between the chain-shift scenario and a competing transparent scenario.

Another way to look at the difference between the chain-shift scenario and the transparent scenario is in terms of output ambiguity. As was discussed in previous sections, rounding in the chain-shift scenario in comparison to the transparent scenario reduces the number of outputs that correspond to inputs distinct in length.

In the chain-shift scenario there is only one output ambiguous in length, the [oi] output. In the transparent scenario, on the other hand, there are two such outputs, [ai] and [oi].

In the following discussion, I will first explain why shortening takes place and then account for rounding. Let us compare the chain-shift scenario to the identity scenario shown below. The identity scenario does not merge any contrasts, and thus wins on PC constraints, but it contains long vowels in the output.[15]

(2-46) Identity scenario

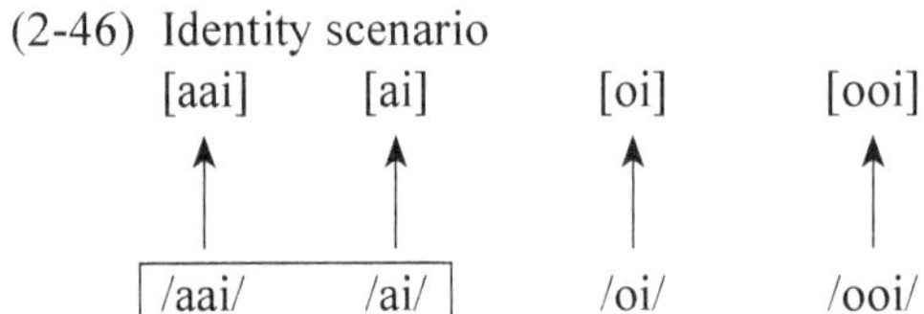

For the chain-shift scenario to win over the identity scenario, it must be essential for long vowels to shorten.

Following Harrikari (2000), I propose that in Finnish shortening takes place to avoid tri-moraic syllables. Some length contrasts are neutralized as a result. In terms of a constraint ranking, a markedness constraint against tri-moraic syllables, $*\sigma_{\mu\mu\mu}$, must outrank conflicting PC constraints against length mergers, PC_{OUT}(long) and PC_{IN}(long). The relevant markedness constraint and the constraint ranking that accounts for shortening are given below.

(2-47) a. $*\sigma_{\mu\mu\mu}$ (Harrikari 2000)
Do not have syllables of three nuclear moras.

b. $*\sigma_{\mu\mu\mu}$ >> PC_{OUT}(long), PC_{IN}(long)

This is illustrated in the following tableau. For clarity of exposition, in the following tableau I list each violation of a constraint as a star and I also indicate next to it a form or a pair of forms that incurs the violation. Markedness is evaluated for each output form in a scenario, and the forms in square brackets are the outputs that violate a particular markedness constraint. For output-oriented PC, the form in square brackets is the output that corresponds to inputs contrasting in length. For input-oriented PC, the pair in curly brackets is the pair that neutralizes length.

Scenarios in the candidate set are formed as described in section 2.2.1. All scenarios in the same candidate set contain the same inputs. Scenario-inputs are generated by a function Gen (similar to the role of Gen in Correspondence Theory). For an underlying form *vapaa-i-na*, and any other form of that length, scenario-inputs contain all strings of length 0–13 (I assume that long vowels count as one segment). Thus, scenario-inputs for that underlying form contain forms such as *vapaa-i-na* (identity form), *vapa-i-na* (by shortening), *vabaa-i-na* (by voicing), *vaba-i-na* (by shortening and voicing), and so on. The forms shown in (2-48) are a subset of these. They are minimally contrastive on vowel length and vowel rounding. Outputs in the scenarios are a subset (possibly improper) of the input. In the identity scenario, the forms in the output are identical to the forms in the input. In the actual scenario and in the total merger scenario, they constitute a proper subset of the input.

(2-48) Shortening takes place

Scenarios		$*\sigma_{\mu\mu\mu}$	PC_{OUT} (long)	PC_{IN} (long)
(i) Identity aai ai ooi oi	/vap**aa**-i-na/ → vap**aa**-i-na /vap**a**-i-na/ → vap**a**-i-na /vap**oo**-i-na/ → vap**oo**-i-na /vap**o**-i-na/ → vap**o**-i-na	**! [aai], [ooi]		
(ii) Actual ☞ aai → ai ↓ ooi → oi	/vap**aa**-i-na/ → vap**a**-i-na /vap**a**-i-na/ → vap**o**-i-na /vap**oo**-i-na/ → vap**o**-i-na /vap**o**-i-na/ → vap**o**-i-na		* [oi]	** {/ai/, /ooi/} {/oi/, /ooi/}
(iii) Total merger aai ai ↘ ↓ ooi → oi	/vap**aa**-i-na/ → vap**o**-i-na /vap**a**-i-na/ → vap**o**-i-na /vap**oo**-i-na/ → vap**o**-i-na /vap**o**-i-na/ → vap**o**-i-na		* [oi]	****! {/ai/, /ooi/} {/oi/, /ooi/} {/ai/, /aai/} {/oi/, /aai/}

The identity scenario, scenario (i), loses on markedness since it contains tri-moraic syllables. The other two scenarios, the actual scenario and the total-merger scenario, both satisfy markedness, but the total-merger scenario incurs too many mergers of length. It merges length for four input pairs. Scenario (ii) is optimal. It merges length but for fewer pairs than the total-merger scenario. In this scenario only two input pairs merge in length.

The ranking so far explains why shortening takes place but it does not account for rounding. Compare the actual scenario to a scenario with shortening but no rounding, the transparent scenario (2-49). In both, there is shortening at the cost of neutralizing length. But in the actual scenario there is also rounding and thus some rounding contrasts are neutralized in addition to length contrasts. Neutralizations of length and rounding contrasts in the actual scenario and in the competing transparent scenario are evaluated below.

(2-49) Input-oriented PC

Scenarios		PC_{IN} (long)	PC_{IN} (round)
(i) Actual aai → ai ↓ ooi → oi	/vap**aa**-i-na/ → vap**a**-i-na /vap**a**-i-na/ → vap**o**-i-na /vap**oo**-i-na/ → vap**o**-i-na /vap**o**-i-na/ → vap**o**-i-na	** {/oi/, /ooi/} {/ai/, /ooi/}	** {/ai/, /oi/} {/ai/, /ooi/}
(ii) Transparent aai → ai ooi → oi	/vap**aa**-i-na/ → vap**a**-i-na /vap**a**-i-na/ → vap**a**-i-na /vap**oo**-i-na/ → vap**o**-i-na /vap**o**-i-na/ → vap**o**-i-na	** {/aai/, /ai/} {/ooi/, /oi/}	

In both scenarios length is merged for the same number of input pairs, but in the actual scenario in addition there are mergers of rounding. In the following discussion, I will explain what forces rounding in the actual scenario and how it aids length contrasts.

Observe that rounding improves on the distribution of length neutralizations in a scenario. In the actual scenario, due to rounding, length mergers are accumulated locally rather than distributed across outputs. As a result, there is an output that does not participate in any length mergers (in fact it does not participate in any merger at all), and thus stands in a bi-unique relation to its input. Thus, rounding reduces the number of ambiguous outputs in a scenario. If we take the number of ambiguous outputs to be an indication of the recoverability of a scenario, rounding improves recoverability (Gussmann 1976, Kaye 1974, 1975, Kisseberth 1976, among others).

For the actual scenario to win, it must be more important to improve on the distribution of length neutralizations in a scenario (contributing to bi-uniqueness) than to avoid merging rounding. This is what forces rounding in Finnish.

(2-50) PC_{OUT}(long) >> PC_{IN}(round), PC_{OUT}(round)

This is illustrated in the following tableau.

(2-51) Vowel rounding takes place

Scenarios		$*\sigma_{\mu\mu\mu}$	PC_{IN} (long)	PC_{OUT} (long)	PC_{IN} (round)	PC_{OUT} (round)
(i) Actual ☞ aai → ai ↓ ooi → oi	/vap**aa**-i-na/ → vap**a**-i-na /vap**a**-i-na/ → vap**o**-i-na /vap**oo**-i-na/ → vap**o**-i-na /vap**o**-i-na/ → vap**o**-i-na		** {/oi/, /ooi/} {/ai/, /ooi/}	* [oi]	** {/ai/, /oi/} {/ai/, /ooi/}	* [oi]
(ii) Transparent aai → ai ooi → oi	/vap**aa**-i-na/ → vap**a**-i-na /vap**a**-i-na/ → vap**a**-i-na /vap**oo**-i-na/ → vap**o**-i-na /vap**o**-i-na/ → vap**o**-i-na		** {/aai/, /ai/} {/ooi/, /oi/}	**! [ai] [oi]		

The actual scenario, with rounding, wins on PC_{OUT}(long). It contains only one output ambiguous in length, whereas the transparent scenario contains two such outputs.

To explain rounding in Finnish, Harrikari (2000) and Anttila (2000) propose a high-ranking markedness constraint against diphthongs of the form *ai*. Harrikari formalizes it as a constraint against nuclei with maximal contour outside of the head syllable, *[MAXCONT]$_{Nuc(Non-H)}$. In PC theory, though the *ai constraint is required to make all distinctions between scenarios in the same candidate set (see the following sections), it is dominated by conflicting PC. Rounding takes place as a result of shortening together with the requirement on preserving contrast. One additional argument in favor of the PC proposal is that *ai* diphthongs are presumably among the most common diphthongs across languages (Kubozono 2001).

As shown in the literature (Harrikari 2000, Karlsson 1999), in Finnish rounding takes place in contexts where shortening occurs, that is in bisyllabic words before the plural and past tense markers. To account for this observation, I have proposed that rounding takes place to preserve contrast. [16]

The constraint ranking established in this section is summarized below. Ranking arguments follow.

(2-52) Constraint ranking

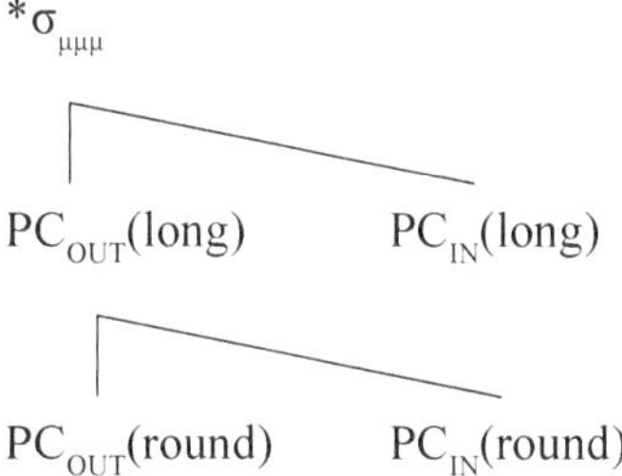

(2-53) Ranking arguments

Ranking	**Consequence**
$*\sigma_{\mu\mu\mu}$ >> PC_{OUT}(long), PC_{IN}(long)	Long vowels are avoided at the cost of merging length.
PC_{OUT}(long) >> PC_{OUT}(round), PC_{IN}(round)	Length neutralizations are accumulated in a scenario by merging rounding.

Recall that shortening takes place to avoid tri-moraic syllables. Due to shortening, some length contrasts are merged ($*\sigma_{\mu\mu\mu}$ >> PC_{OUT}(long), PC_{IN}(long)). But length mergers need to be well distributed (accumulated locally) in a scenario, and this is at the cost of merging rounding (PC_{OUT}(long) >> PC_{OUT}(round), PC_{IN}(round)). As a result, rounding takes place. Formally, rounding is an indirect consequence of shortening and a high-ranked requirement on the accumulation of length neutralizations in a scenario.

The chain-shift scenario preserves some length contrasts despite shortening. Length contrast is preserved for one minimal pair of inputs in a scenario, /aai/ vs. /ai/, and is manifested as a surface rounding contrast. Thus, *contrast transformation* takes place.[17]

Below is the general chain shift schema in cases like Finnish:

(2-54) Chain shift schema (cf. (2-52))

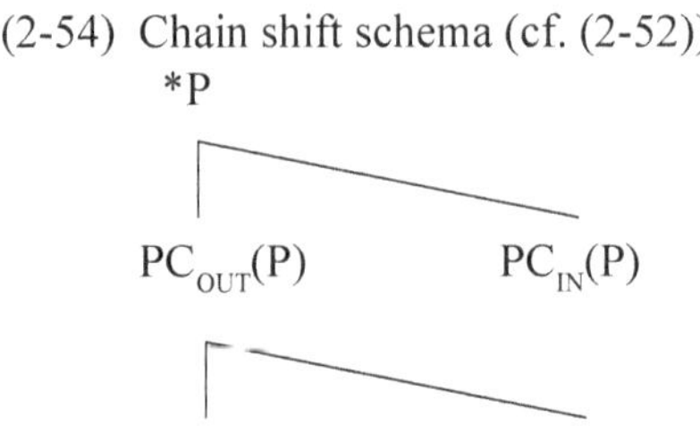

P-type segments are avoided due to high-ranked markedness and this results in some P mergers (*P >> PC_{OUT}(P), PC_{IN}(P)). But there is a high-ranking requirement on the distribution of P mergers in a scenario: output-oriented PC. It requires that fewer outputs correspond to inputs contrasting in P. That forces Q mergers, as only by merging along some other dimension of contrast can the contrast distribution requirement be satisfied as much as possible (PC_{OUT}(P) >> PC_{OUT}(Q), PC_{IN}(Q)). In effect, some original instances of the P contrast are preserved on the surface and manifested as contrast Q. Some instances of the Q contrast are lost.

This illustrates an important prediction of PC theory. In PC theory, a phonological process can take place solely to improve on the distribution of some contrast in a scenario. In the schematic example above, P distribution is improved by Q mergers. To improve P distribution means to accumulate neutralizations of P in one location in a scenario rather than distributing them among outputs. As a result, fewer outputs are ambiguous in P. This is the role of output-oriented PC. The high-ranking PC_{OUT}(P) constraint forces a phonological process (the Q process). This shows that PC constraints can activate a phonological process without reference to a high-ranking markedness constraint as long as there is a markedness constraint that initiates the shift.[18]

2.5 Factorial typology

This section discusses factorial typology, which is an essential aspect of any OT analysis. It provides a set of scenarios predicted by the ranking permutations of the proposed constraints and shows whether they are attested cross-linguistically. It also shows that the actual scenario wins from among its competitors under the established constraint ranking.

The following discussion considers scenarios in a candidate set that consists of inputs minimally distinct in vowel length and vowel rounding {/aai/, /ai/, /oi/, /ooi/}.[19] As described in section 2.2.1, all scenarios in a given candidate set contain the same inputs but differ in the set of outputs and/or input–output relations. Outputs are a subset of the inputs. Two of the four inputs cannot be used as outputs, as they violate high-ranked markedness against tri-moraic syllables and would lose to any other scenario in Finnish. Thus, the only outputs that are considered are {[ai], [oi]}.

Altogether, there are 16 logically possible scenarios. Below is the set of logically possible scenarios involving the four inputs. Scenarios are labeled according to the types of mappings they contain. Some labels are familiar, others will be explained as we go along. Row one starts with scenarios where rounding applies transparently: there is either no rounding (scenario (i)), or rounding or lowering applies to all forms subject to it (scenarios (ii), and (iii)). The next two cells present bi-directional scenarios – those involve both rounding and lowering. These are followed by cross-corner scenarios where vowels both shorten and change in rounding. Chain shifts and derived environment effects are represented in row three. They are examples of opaque scenarios. Row four shows scenarios that involve movement in various directions, thus called multi-directional. Scenarios called reverse constitute a mirror image of an immediately preceding scenario. Unattested scenarios are shaded.

(2-55) Full typology (given top-ranked $*\sigma_{\mu\mu\mu}$)

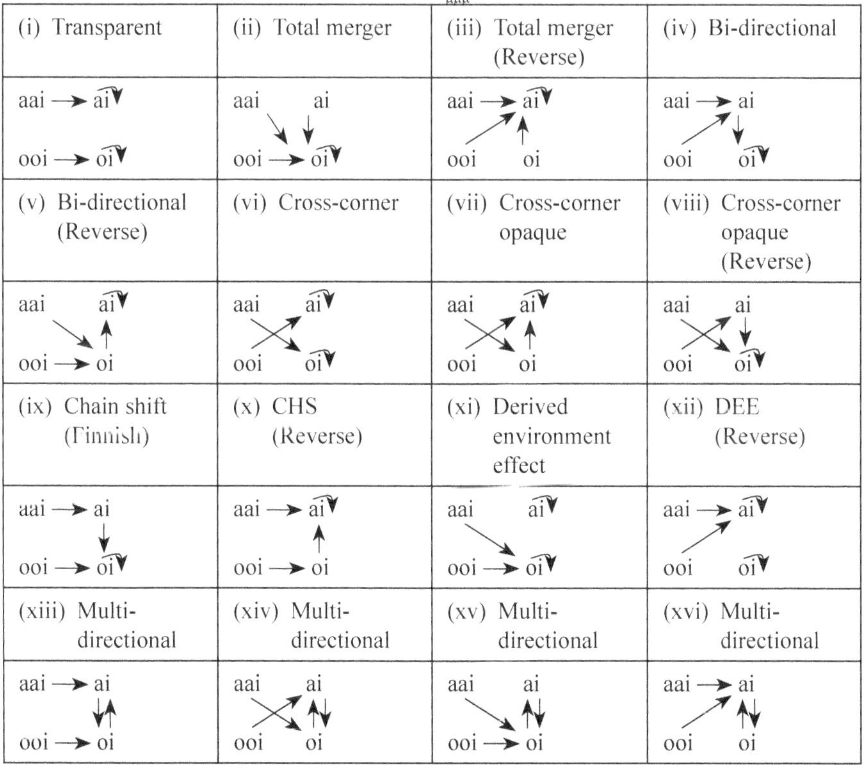

(i) Transparent	(ii) Total merger	(iii) Total merger (Reverse)	(iv) Bi-directional
aai → a͡i✓ ooi → o͡i✓	aai ai ooi → o͡i✓	aai → a͡i✓ ooi oi	aai → ai ooi o͡i✓
(v) Bi-directional (Reverse)	(vi) Cross-corner	(vii) Cross-corner opaque	(viii) Cross-corner opaque (Reverse)
aai a͡i✓ ooi → oi	aai a͡i✓ ooi o͡i✓	aai a͡i✓ ooi oi	aai ai ooi o͡i✓
(ix) Chain shift (Finnish)	(x) CHS (Reverse)	(xi) Derived environment effect	(xii) DEE (Reverse)
aai → ai ooi → o͡i✓	aai → a͡i✓ ooi → oi	aai a͡i✓ ooi → o͡i✓	aai → a͡i✓ ooi o͡i✓
(xiii) Multi-directional	(xiv) Multi-directional	(xv) Multi-directional	(xvi) Multi-directional
aai → ai ooi → oi	aai ai ooi oi	aai ai ooi → oi	aai → ai ooi oi

The actual scenario in Finnish is the chain-shift scenario, scenario (ix) (row three). A competing transparent scenario with no rounding is shown in (i) (top left).

Some of the scenarios are unattested. In OT, this means that there exists no constraint ranking under which a mapping would win. Such mapping is then harmonically bounded by its competitors.

As will be explained below, seven scenarios are harmonically bounded by the remaining scenarios and will never come out as optimal. Scenarios are harmonically bounded either on PC in stage 1 of Eval (this is when they merge too many types of contrasts, involve too many input pairs in a merger, or contain too many ambiguous outputs), or on faithfulness in stage 2 of Eval (this is when they involve too much movement). Arguments for harmonic bounding are given below.[20]

(2-56) Arguments for harmonic bounding

(a) In (2-55), the cross-corner scenarios (vii) and (viii), and multi-directional scenarios (xv) and (xvi), are harmonically bounded by the opaque scenarios, (ix) through (xii). They involve the same PC and markedness violations as the competing opaque scenarios but contain too much movement. That is, in these scenarios outputs and their corresponding inputs are too different from each other. Thus, these scenarios are harmonically bounded on FAITHFULNESS in stage 2 of Eval. The relevant tableaux follow. The scenarios with rounding are presented first, followed by the ones with lowering.

Fewer unfaithful [ai]'s (=rounding)

	$*\sigma_{\mu\mu\mu}$	PC_{REL} (rd)	PC_{OUT} (lg)	PC_{IN} (lg)	PC_{OUT} (rd)	PC_{IN} (rd)	*ai	*oi	(-rd) FAITH	(+rd) FAITH
(viii) Cross-cor.			*	**	*	**	*	***	**	***
(ix) CHS			*	**	*	**	*	***	*	**
(xi) DEE			*	**	*	**	*	***		***
(xv) Multi-dir.			*	**	*	**	*	***	*	****

Fewer unfaithful [oi]'s (=lowering)

	$*\sigma_{\mu\mu\mu}$	PC_{REL} (rd)	PC_{OUT} (lg)	PC_{IN} (lg)	PC_{OUT} (rd)	PC_{IN} (rd)	*ai	*oi	(-rd) FAITH	(+rd) FAITH
(vii) Cross-cor.			*	**	*	**	***	*	***	**
(x) CHS (Reverse)			*	**	*	**	***	*	**	*
(xii) DEE (Reverse)			*	**	*	**	***	*	***	
(xvi) Multi-dir.			*	**	*	**	***	*	****	*

This shows that in PC theory, when scenarios tie on PC and markedness in stage 1 of Eval (see above), faithfulness in stage 2 chooses in favor of a scenario where inputs are overall closer to their outputs.

(b) Similarly, the multi-directional scenario (xiv) is harmonically bounded by the transparent scenario (i) on FAITHFULNESS.

	$*\sigma_{\mu\mu\mu}$	PC_{REL} (rd)	PC_{OUT} (lg)	PC_{IN} (lg)	PC_{OUT} (rd)	PC_{IN} (rd)	*ai	*oi	(-rd) FAITH	(+rd) FAITH
(i) Transparent			**	**			**	**	*	*
(xiv) Multi-dir.			**	**			**	**	***	***

The two scenarios incur the same PC and markedness violations (stage 1 of Eval), but the multi-directional scenario violates faithfulness too much (stage 2), and thus will never win over the competing transparent scenario.

(c) Finally, the cross-corner scenario (vi) and the multi-directional scenario (xiii) are harmonically bounded by the transparent scenario (i) even before FAITHFULNESS comes into play. They fare the same on markedness but violate too many types of PC constraints.

	$*\sigma_{\mu\mu\mu}$	PC_{REL} (rd)	PC_{OUT} (lg)	PC_{IN} (lg)	PC_{OUT} (rd)	PC_{IN} (rd)	*ai	*oi	(-rd) FAITH	(+rd) FAITH
(i) Transparent			**	**			**	**	*	*
(vi) Cross-cor.			**	**	**	**	**	**	**	**
(xiii) Multi-dir.			**	**	**	**	**	**	**	**

The transparent scenario merges along fewer dimensions of contrast (it does not violate PC(round) constraints at all), and thus wins over the two competing scenarios, regardless of the constraint ranking.

We are left with nine scenarios that have a chance to win. I will refer to them as predicted scenarios. A summary tableau of constraint violations in Finnish is given in the Appendix (A.1).

The following table shows the set of predicted scenarios. Harmonically bounded scenarios have been excluded. To the best of my knowledge, this prediction coincides with the set of empirically attested phenomena.[21]

(2-57) Predicted scenarios

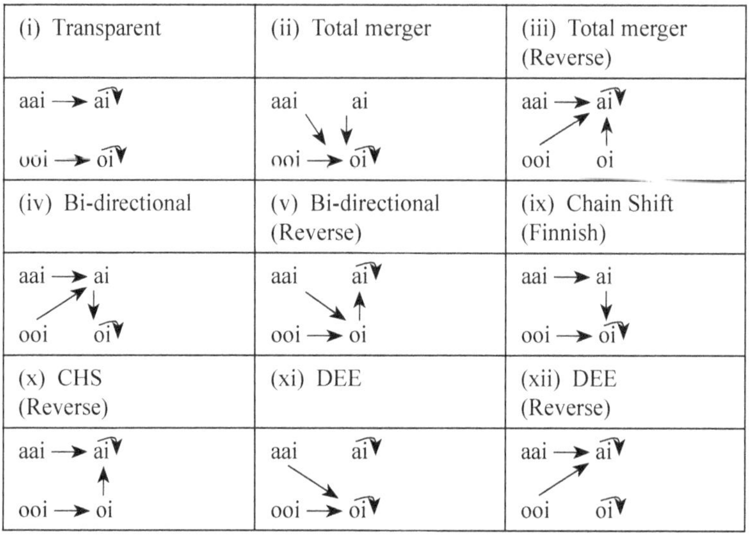

(i) Transparent	(ii) Total merger	(iii) Total merger (Reverse)
aai → ai✓ ooi → oi✓	aai ai ↘ ↓ ooi → oi✓	aai → ai✓ ↗ ↑ ooi oi
(iv) Bi-directional	(v) Bi-directional (Reverse)	(ix) Chain Shift (Finnish)
aai → ai ↗ ↓ ooi oi✓	aai ai✓ ↘ ↑ ooi → oi	aai → ai ↓ ooi → oi✓
(x) CHS (Reverse)	(xi) DEE	(xii) DEE (Reverse)
aai → ai✓ ↑ ooi → oi	aai ai✓ ↘ ooi → oi✓	aai → ai✓ ↗ ooi oi✓

Examples of chain shifts and derived environment effects can be found in Kean (1974), Kiparsky (1982, 1993), Kirchner (1996), Łubowicz (2002), Mascaró (1976), McCarthy (1999), and Rubach (1984), among others.

An example of a bi-directional scenario comes from the history of nasal vowels in Polish (Rospond 1971, Rothstein 1993). In the history of Polish, some nasal vowels lowered, others raised. As reported by Rospond 1971 and Rothstein 1993, lowering applied to underlying long nasal vowels (2-58a), and raising targeted their short counterparts (2-58b).[22]

(2-58) a. Lowering (and shortening) (nom.sg.masc.)

ę: > ą	*r[ę:]d	>	rz[ą]d	'row'
ą: > ą	* m[ą:]ż	>	m[ą]ż	'husband'

b. Raising (gen.sg.masc.)

ę > ę	* r[ę]du	>	rz[ę]du	'row'
ą > ę	* m[ą]ża	>	m[ę]ża	'husband'

As a result, contrast was preserved between underlying short and long nasal vowels. The two kinds mapped onto distinct outputs. Long nasal vowels mapped onto low vowels (2-58a). Short nasal vowels mapped onto mid vowels (2-58b). This is shown below.

(2-59) Bi-directional scenario

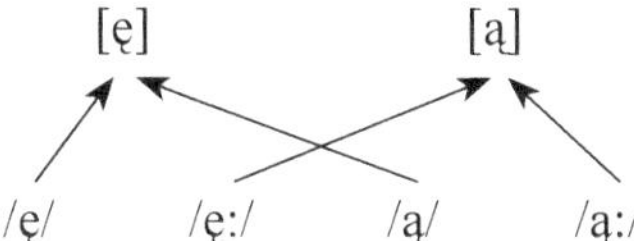

The bi-directional scenario posits an underlying opposition that does not have any surface correlates (absolute neutralization). The bi-directional scenario contains an output height contrast that does not correspond to any minimal instances of an input height contrast.[23]

Finally, it is shown that the established constraint ranking selects the Finnish scenario as optimal. This is illustrated below.

(2-60) Ranking for Finnish (assuming high-ranked $*\sigma_{\mu\mu\mu}$)

	PC_{REL} (rd)	PC_{OUT} (long)	PC_{IN} (long)	PC_{OUT} (rd)	PC_{IN} (rd)	*ai	*oi	(+rd)-FAITH	(-rd)-FAITH
(i) Transp.		**!	**			**	**	*	*
(ii) Total merger		*	****!	*	****		****	****	
(iii) Total merger (Reverse)		*	****!	*	****	****			****
(iv) Bi-directional	*!			**	**	**	**	*	***
(v) Bi-directional (Reverse)	*!			**	**	**	**	***	*
(ix) CHS ☞		*	**	*	**	*	***	**	*
(x) CHS (Reverse)		*	**	*	**	***!	*	*	**
(xi) DEE		*	**	*	**	*	***	***!	
(xii) DEE (Reverse)		*	**	*	**	***!	*		***

The transparent scenario, scenario (i), loses on output-oriented PC, PC_{OUT}(long). It contains too many outputs that are ambiguous in length. The total merger scenarios, scenarios (ii) and (iii), lose on PC_{IN}(long), as they both merge too many input pairs that are distinct in length. The bi-directional scenarios, scenarios (iv) and (v), are ruled out on PC_{REL}(round) since in those scenarios none of the minimal input rounding contrasts are preserved in the output. The opaque scenarios with lowering, scenarios (x) and (xii), are ruled out on markedness *ai since they contain too many tokens of unrounded vowels. The remaining two scenarios, scenario (ix) and (xi), pass on to stage 2 of Eval. In stage 2, the scenario where rounded vowels are more faithful, scenario (ix), wins.

The proposed constraints also generate the remaining attested scenarios, as shown below. That is, each of the empirically attested scenarios from the candidate set is predicted to win in some language.

(2-61) Factorial typology

Stage 1 of Evaluation	Stage 2 of Evaluation
Transparent (scenario (i)): $*\sigma_{\mu\mu\mu}$, $PC_{OUT/IN}$(rd) >> $PC_{OUT/IN}$(lg), *ai, *oi	
Total merger onto [oi] (scenario (ii)): *ai >> PC, *oi	
Total merger onto [ai] (scenario (iii)): *oi >> PC, *ai	
Bi-directional: $*\sigma_{\mu\mu\mu}$, $PC_{OUT/IN}$(lg) >> $PC_{OUT/IN}$(rd), *ai, *oi, PC_{REL}(rd)	Fewer mergers onto [oi] (scenario (iv)): (+rd)-Faith>>(-rd)-Faith
	Fewer mergers onto [ai] (scenario (v)): (-rd)-Faith>>(+rd)-Faith
Opaque (with rounding): $*\sigma_{\mu\mu\mu}$,PC_{REL}(rd)>>$PC_{OUT/IN}$(lg)>>$PC_{OUT/IN}$(rd),*ai>>*oi	Fewer mergers onto [oi] (scenario (ix)): (+rd)-Faith>>(-rd)-Faith
	Fewer mergers onto [ai] (scenario (xi)): (-rd)-Faith>>(+rd)-Faith
Opaque (with lowering): $*\sigma_{\mu\mu\mu}$,PC_{REL}(rd)>>$PC_{OUT/IN}$(lg)>>$PC_{OUT/IN}$(rd),*oi>>*ai	Fewer mergers onto [oi] (scenario (x)): (-rd)-Faith>>(+rd)-Faith
	Fewer mergers onto [ai] (scenario (xii)): (+rd)-Faith>>(-rd)-Faith

All distinctions are made among scenarios. This shows that our constraint inventory generates all of the attested scenario types – a basic goal of OT.

2.6 Predictions

This section discusses predictions of PC theory and compares them to previous approaches. Unlike previous approaches, PC theory admits push shift mappings. Similar to previous approaches, it rules out pull shifts and circular shifts with no termination point, and admits regular shifts. The predictions of PC theory are discussed below.

2.6.1 PC constraints as faithfulness and markedness

In standard OT phonological mappings are accounted for by the relative ranking of markedness and faithfulness constraints. Markedness constraints demand output well-formedness. Faithfulness constraints call for input–output identity. The two often conflict and their conflict is resolved by constraint ranking. When markedness outranks conflicting faithfulness, a phonological process takes place. With the opposite ranking, a phonological process is blocked.

In PC theory some of the role previously assigned to markedness and faithfulness constraints is taken over by novel PC constraints. As will be explained below, PC constraints infringe on the territory previously assigned to markedness and faithfulness. Since PC constraints take on some of the role of both markedness and faithfulness, they somewhat blur the distinction between the two seemingly distinct families of constraints. Let us consider the dual nature of PC constraints.

PC as faithfulness. Standard faithfulness requires input–output identity in a particular phonological property. Thus, when ranked above conflicting markedness, faithfulness constraints block a phonological process. Like standard faithfulness, PC constraints block a phonological process when ranked higher than conflicting markedness and allow it to apply with the opposite ranking. This was shown in section 2.3 with the example of final devoicing. When PC against the voicing merger outranked markedness against voiced obstruents syllable-finally, final devoicing was blocked. It was more important to preserve the voicing contrast than to satisfy markedness. When, on the other hand, markedness was ranked higher than the conflicting PC constraint, final devoicing took place. Markedness satisfaction was the top priority. The rankings for neutralization and the lack of it are recalled below.

(2-62) Neutralization and the lack of it

Final devoicing	$*\text{VOICEDOBSTRUENT}]_\sigma >> \text{PC}_{\text{IN}}(\text{voice}), \text{PC}_{\text{OUT}}(\text{voice})$
No devoicing	$\text{PC}_{\text{IN}}(\text{voice}), \text{PC}_{\text{OUT}}(\text{voice}) >> *\text{VOICEDOBSTRUENT}]_\sigma$

Both PC constraints and standard faithfulness ensure contrast preservation but only PC constraints allow for contrast transformation. PC constraints are satisfied even when a given underlying contrast is transformed into a different surface contrast. Standard faithfulness does not allow for that. Thus, if the obstruent voicing contrast is manifested by contrast in vowel length, PC constraints are satisfied but standard faithfulness constraints are violated.

In other words, standard faithfulness constraints do not distinguish between the loss and transformation of a phonological property, treating both as violations of faithfulness constraints. PC constraints, on the other hand, favor transformation to the loss of contrast. One can then ask whether in PC theory contrast transformation is not always better than the loss of contrast. After all, transformation preserves contrast. But transformation has consequences for a system of mappings. Transformation results in additional mergers, some of which may be disallowed in a given grammar. These are some of the differences between PC and standard faithfulness. Let us now move on to the discussion of PC as markedness.

PC as markedness. Markedness constraints are constraints on output well-formedness. When ranked higher than conflicting faithfulness, they force a phonological process. PC constraints take on some of the role of markedness, in that they are able to activate a phonological process. In section 2.4 we have seen an example of a Finnish chain shift, where the latter process in the shift, the process of rounding, is forced by a high-ranking PC constraint on the accumulation of length mergers in a scenario. The relevant ranking is recalled below.

(2-63) Chain shift rankings
Finnish $*\sigma_{\mu\mu\mu}$ >> PC_{OUT}(long) >> PC_{OUT}(round), PC_{IN}(round)

Unlike standard markedness, PC constraints can only activate a phonological process when there is another mapping that takes place in the system. In a chain-shift scenario, PC constraints can only force the latter mapping in the shift. The initial mapping has to take place for reasons of output well-formedness.

Thus we have seen that PC constraints act like both markedness and faithfulness constraints in standard OT. They combine the properties of the two previously distinct forces in the grammatical system. This double identity of PC constraints follows from the architecture of PC theory and allows us to provide a uniform explanation of opaque and transparent processes.

Generalized faithfulness. In PC theory, faithfulness constraints are required to rule out unnecessary movement. This becomes relevant when two scenarios tie on PC and markedness, but one of the scenarios involves too much disparity between its inputs and corresponding outputs. Faithfulness then rules in favor of the scenario where outputs are overall closer to their inputs. Generalized faithfulness is also necessary to determine directionality of movement in a scenario.

Tokenized markedness. Markedness constraints in PC are indispensable to ignite a shift. As we have seen in Finnish, if there were no high-ranking markedness against tri-moraic syllables, there would be no shift – no shortening and thus no rounding. PC by itself can force the latter step in the shift, such as rounding, but it cannot force the initial step, such as shortening. Only markedness can do so. Tokenized markedness also determines the directionality of movement in a scenario.

2.6.2 Typology of chain shifts in PC theory

This section discusses the predictions of PC theory with respect to chain shifts and compares them with previous approaches. One of the key predictions is that unlike previous approaches, PC theory admits push shift mappings.

Assume that /A/ maps onto [B] (A→B) and /B/ maps onto [C] (B→C) but crucially /A/ does not become [C]. Thus, there is a chain shift effect of the form: A→B→C. One type of chain shift is a push shift mapping. In a phonological push shift, the latter step in the shift, /B/→[C], is a consequence of the prior step, /A/→[B], and not an independently motivated phonological process (see Ahn 2004, Barrie 2006, Hsieh 2005, Labov 1994, Maclagan and Hay 2004, Martinet 1952, 1955, Miglio and Morén 2003, and Schendl and Ritt 2002, among others).

Some examples of push shifts described in the literature include: Swedish shift (Benediktsson 1970, Labov 1994): a → a: → ɔ : → o: → u: → ü; New Zealand shift (Bauer 1979, 1992, Gordon *et al.* 2004, Maclagan and Hay 2004, Trudgill *et al.* 1998): æ → e → i → ei/ɨ; Northern Cities Shift (Labov 1994): e → ʌ → oh; Great Vowel Shift (Luick 1914, Miglio and Morén 2003, Minkova and Stockwell 2003): ɛ: → e: → i: → ai, ɔ: → o: → u: → au, Short Vowel Shift (Lass 1999, Schendl and Ritt 2002): u → o → ɔ → ɒ, a → æ, and tone sandhi described below.

To argue that A→B→C is a push shift mapping, one must show that there is no markedness constraint that favors [C] over [B], and thus no independent motivation for the latter mapping in the shift. In addition, one must establish that the mapping /B/→[C] is always linked with /A/→[B] and that there is, therefore, a causal relation between the mappings in the shift.

Consider tone sandhi in Xiamen, a dialect of the Min language of the Sino-Tibetan family (see Barrie 2006, Chen 1987). The diagram below uses the following notation: [U] means upper register, [L] lower register, [lh] rising pitch, and [hl] falling pitch. Thus, for example, [U, lh] is a high-rising tone where the pitch moves from the low end of the upper register to the high end.

(2-64) Xiamen tone sandhi

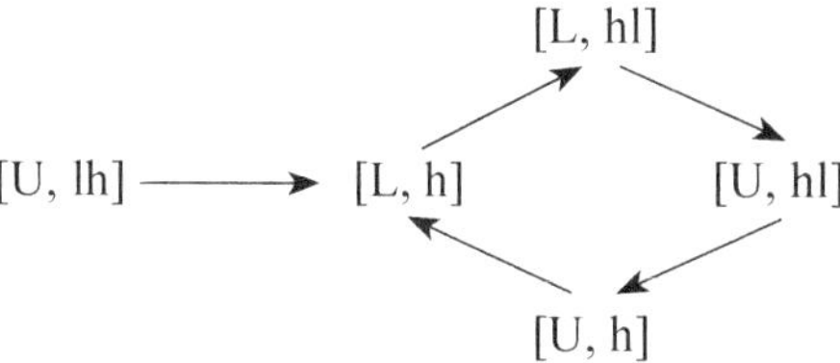

Barrie observes that the above tonal shift is an example of a push shift mapping: the initial mapping in the shift is due to markedness improvement, such as avoidance of rising tones (*[U, lh]). However, the subsequent mapping of [L, h] onto [L, hl] does not improve on markedness since it creates a contour tone from an input level tone, and research on tonal markedness has shown that contour tones are more marked than level tones (see Alderete 1999, Yip 2004, Zoll 1997, among others). In view of this, Barrie proposes that the latter step in the shift, [L, h]→[L, hl], is a result of the initial step, [U, lh]→[L, h], and the need to maintain contrast between tones of various registers. In other words, due to the chain shift effect the input tones [U, lh] and [L, h] map onto [L, h] and [L, hl], respectively. Otherwise, if there was no shift both input tones would map onto [L, h]. Since the latter step in the shift, [L, h]→[L, hl], is not due to markedness improvement and the latter step is always linked with the prior step, this is an example of a push shift mapping. The remaining mappings in the shift are analyzed in a similar manner (for a complete analysis see Barrie 2006). See also Hsieh (2005).[24]

Push shifts are problematic to rule-based approaches to phonology and initially to OT. In rule-based approaches chain shifts are accounted for by rule ordering. But in a push shift mapping, there is no separate rule that accounts for the latter step in the shift. The latter step in a push shift mapping is a consequence of the prior step and not an independently motivated phonological process. In consequence, push shifts are not admitted under a rule-based analysis.[25]

Similarly, push shifts are initially problematic to OT. OT approaches to chain shifts include local conjunction (Kirchner 1996) and ternary scales (Gnanadesikan 1997) as well as more general accounts of opacity in OT, such as sympathy theory (McCarthy 1999, 2003a), stratal OT (also known as LPM-OT) (Kiparsky 2000), output–output correspondence (Benua 1997, Burzio 1998), targeted constraints (Wilson 2001), comparative markedness (McCarthy 2003b), turbidity (Goldrick and Smolensky 1999), and candidate chain theory (McCarthy 2007), among others. But unlike PC theory, none of the accounts admit push shifts because they all require that there exists a markedness constraint that triggers /B/→[C]. In OT, a phonological process can only apply if there is a high-ranked markedness constraint against it (Moreton 1996/1999). But in push shifts /B/→[C] is not due to markedness.

To account for chain shifts, Kirchner (1996) proposes special faithfulness constraints in the form of local conjunction (Smolensky 1993, 1997). In this approach, phonological processes involved in the shift must be forced by high-ranking markedness constraints but local conjunction blocks a process from applying if it results in double faithfulness violation in a given domain. Local conjunction is defined below.

(2-65) Definition of local conjunction (Smolensky 1993)
The local conjunction of C_1 and C_2 in domain *D*, $[C_1 \& C_2]_D$, is violated when there is some domain of type *D* in which both C_1 and C_2 are violated.

Thus, if the domain of local conjunction is a segment, both C_1 and C_2 cannot be violated together in the same segment.

In the tonal chain shift represented in (2-64), both the initial step in the shift [U, lh]→[L, h] and the subsequent step [L, h]→[L, hl] would need to be forced by markedness constraints, and local conjunction would prohibit [U, lh] from going all the way to [L, hl]. As already explained, the tonal shift is an example of a push shift mapping. The problem here for the local conjunction approach is that [L, h]→[L, hl] cannot be accounted for by markedness improvement. In summary, the local conjunction proposal would not account for push shifts because in a push shift mapping there is no high-ranked markedness constraint that triggers the second step in the shift.

PC theory proposes a solution to push shift mappings in OT by the use of contrast. The key observation is that the latter step in the shift /B/→[C] is due to contrast and PC theory provides formal tools to incorporate this observation into the grammar. This is illustrated in the following tableau. The tableau compares three scenarios: the push shift scenario, the identity scenario where all inputs map onto identical outputs, and the so-called transparent scenario with no /B/→[C]. The constraint ranking proposed below captures the observation that the initial mapping in the shift /A/→[B] is due to markedness *A but the subsequent mapping /B/→[C] is facilitated by contrast preservation, PC_{IN}(A/B). The relevant ranking is: *A, PC_{IN}(A/B) >> PC_{IN}(B/C).

(2-66) PC theory admits push shifts

	Scenarios	*A	PC_{IN}(A/B)	PC_{IN}(B/C)
(i) Push shift ☞	/A/→ B /B/ → C /C/ → C			*
(ii) Identity	/A/ → A /B/ → B /C/ → C	*!		
(iii) Transparent	/A/ → B /B/ → B /C/ → C		*!	

The identity scenario, scenario (ii), loses on markedness *A. The transparent scenario, scenario (iii), merges contrast, thus violating PC_{IN}(A/B). The push shift scenario, scenario (i), wins under the proposed constraint ranking. In a push shift mapping, the /B/→[C] mapping takes place to preserve contrast between /A/ and /B/. The push shift mapping is initiated by markedness improvement and further facilitated by preserving contrast. Unlike in standard OT, the latter mapping in the shift /B/→[C] does not need to be due to a high-ranked markedness *B. The assumption here is that in a push shift such a markedness constraint either does not exist or is ranked below PC_{IN}(A/B).[26]

PC theory explains tone sandhi (see (2-64)) in the same way (Barrie 2006). It proposes that the latter mapping in the shift, [L, h] onto [L, hl], takes place because a prior mapping, [U, lh] onto [L, h], improves on markedness, and there is a requirement on preserving contrast between tones of various registers, [U] and [L]. The latter step in the shift is a consequence of the prior step and not an independently motivated phonological process.

Thus, PC theory provides a formal way to incorporate push shifts into the grammar. The core of the proposal is the use of contrast as an imperative in a phonological system. In the rest of this section, I will consider predictions of PC theory for other kinds of shifts, such as pull shifts, regular shifts, and circular shifts, and compare them to previous approaches.

Pull shifts. Unlike push shifts, pull shift mappings are ruled out in all approaches to chain shifts. In a pull shift mapping, also known as a drag shift, the prior step in the shift, /A/→[B], takes place not due to markedness but because the latter step, /B/→[C], occurs (King 1969). In some sense, pull shifts are a mirror image of a push shift mapping. In rule-based approaches to chain shifts, pull shifts are not admitted because there is no separate rule that accounts for the initial step in the shift. In standard OT, similarly, pull shifts are not admitted since the initial mapping in the shift is not forced by markedness and thus is not predicted to occur. As will be shown below, PC theory also rules out pull shifts.

Consider A→B→C as an example of a pull shift. The mapping /B/→[C] is forced by markedness *B but the initial mapping /A/→[B] is not. This is illustrated in the following tableau. I compare a pull shift scenario, scenario (ii), to a no shift scenario, scenario (i), under the constraint ranking: $PC_{IN/OUT}$(A/B), *B >> $PC_{IN/OUT}$(B/C). There is no markedness constraint that compels the /A/→[B] mapping.

(2-67) No pull shift

		Scenarios	$PC_{IN/OUT}$(A/B)	*B	$PC_{IN/OUT}$(B/C)
(i) No shift A B → C	☞	/A/ → A /B/ → C /C/ → C			*
(ii) Pull shift A → B → C		/A/ → B /B/ → C /C/ → C		*!	*

Both scenarios preserve contrast between /A/ vs. /B/ because underlying A and B map onto different outputs in both scenarios. Both scenarios map /B/ onto [C] in accordance with markedness *B ranked over PC_{IN}(B/C). But the pull shift scenario incurs a fatal violation of *B.[27]

Thus, PC theory predicts that there exist shifts without a markedness constraint against the intermediate stage (push shifts as shown in (2-66)) but that there are no shifts without a markedness constraint against the initial stage (no pull shifts as shown in (2-67)). Push shifts improve on PC, whereas pull shifts do not, and in addition incur an unmotivated violation of markedness.[28]

Circular shifts. Both standard OT and the contrast approach rule out circular shifts with no termination point, for example /A/→[B] and /B/→[A]. As shown by Moreton (1996/1999), a circular shift is not admitted to non-contrast OT since it does not improve on markedness. Circular shifts are also not admitted to PC theory since they do not improve on contrast, and involve an unmotivated violation of generalized faithfulness. In PC theory, a circular shift is harmonically bounded by a competing identity scenario. Rule-based approaches admit circular shifts with no termination point (see McCarthy 1999 for discussion).

Consider a circular shift scenario and compare it to an identity scenario.

(2-68) No circular shifts – unmotivated violations of faithfulness

	Scenarios	$PC_{IN/OUT}$	PC_{REL}	MARK	FAITH
(i) Circular shift A B ↑↓ ↓↑ D C	/A/ → D /B/ → C /C/ → B /D/ → A			A,B,C,D	****! A→D B→C C→B D→A
(ii) Identity ☞ A B D C	/A/ → A /B/ → B /C/ → C /D/ → D			A,B,C,D	

Both scenarios satisfy PC constraints and incur the same violations of markedness (they have the same outputs). But the circular shift scenario, scenario (i), is ruled out on generalized faithfulness. There are unmotivated violations of faithfulness in this scenario.

Some instances of circular shifts are also ruled out by relational PC. The following tableau compares the circular shift scenario to an identity scenario.

(2-69) No circular shifts – unnecessary PC_{REL} violations

Scenarios		$PC_{IN/OUT}$	PC_{REL}	MARK	FAITH
(i) Circular shift A → B ↑ ↓ D ← C	/A/ → B /B/ → C /C/ → D /D/ → A		*!	A,B,C,D	**** A→B B→C C→D D→A
(ii) Identity ☞ A B D C	/A/ → A /B/ → B /C/ → C /D/ → D			A,B,C,D	

Both scenarios satisfy input- and output-oriented PC constraints. In both, all input segments map onto distinct outputs and none of the outputs are ambiguous. Both scenarios incur the same violations of markedness since they contain the same outputs and the same number of them. But the circular shift scenario, scenario (i), violates relational PC constraints by permuting contrasts too much. In the circular shift, none of the original minimal input contrasts are preserved in the output (see section 2.5).

To sum up, in PC theory there is no shift unless it improves on PC or markedness. This shows that circular shifts are ruled out in favor of a non-circular mapping (similarly exchange rules; see Anderson and Browne 1973). The same prediction is made in standard OT (Moreton 1996/1999).[29]

Regular shifts. All approaches predict shifts where each mapping in the shift is due to markedness: so-called regular shifts. Rule-based approaches predict regular shifts by rule ordering. Standard OT admits regular shifts by blocking an otherwise regular phonological process by special faithfulness constraints and other means (see section 2.6.1). Similarly, OT with contrast accounts for regular shifts by blocking an otherwise regular phonological process by PC constraints.

Consider a regular chain shift A→B→C where each step in the shift is forced by markedness constraints. But the process /A/→[C] is blocked for underlying /A/ to maintain contrast between underlying /A/ and /B/. The ranking and the relevant tableau are given below. To illustrate PC blocking, I compare a no shift scenario where both /A/ and /B/ map onto [C] with a regular shift of the form A→B→C.

(2-70) PC blocking
$PC_{IN/OUT}$(A/B) >> *B >> $PC_{IN/OUT}$(B/C) (also *A >> *B)

(2-71) Regular shifts exist

	Scenarios	$PC_{IN/OUT}$(A/B)	*B	$PC_{IN/OUT}$(B/C)
(i) No shift A B→C (A→C, C→C)	/A/ → C /B/ → C /C/ → C	*!		*
(ii) Regular shift ☞ A→B→C (C→C)	/A/ → B /B/ → C /C/ → C		*	*

Scenario (i) loses since it merges the contrast between underlying /A/ and /B/. Scenario (ii) wins because in this scenario /A/ and /B/ map onto distinct outputs. This is at the expense of violating markedness *B since $PC_{IN/OUT}$(A/B) outranks *B. Thus, PC theory predicts regular shifts to occur.

To sum up, the key prediction of PC theory is that it admits push shift mappings where the latter step in the shift takes place solely to preserve contrast and is not an independently motivated phonological process. This prediction is crucially different from previous approaches to chain shifts in both standard OT and rule-based phonology. This is because in PC theory, unlike previous approaches, contrast exists as a formal property of the grammar formulated as a set of rankable and violable constraints. The constraints on contrast interact with each other and with other constraints in the grammar resulting in preservation or loss of contrast. Predictions of PC theory with respect to other shifts have also been discussed. PC theory rules out pull shift mappings, and circular shifts with no termination point, but admits regular shifts.

2.7 Dispersion theory

There exists a model of contrast in OT, called the Dispersion Theory of Contrast (henceforth DTC) (Bradley 2001, 2006, Flemming 1995, 1996, 2004, Ito and Mester 2004, 2007, Ní Chiosáin and Padgett 2010, Padgett 1997, 2000, 2001, 2003, Padgett and Zygis 2007, Sanders 2003, among others). Both PC theory introduced in this book and DTC recognize contrast as a formal principle of the grammar and formulate it, albeit in a slightly different form, as a family of rankable and violable constraints. Both PC theory and DTC also recognize that to evaluate contrast, candidates must be sets of forms or mappings rather than individual mappings as in standard OT.

Dispersion Theory is based on the following functional principles (following Lindblom 1986, 1990):

(2-72) Functional principles in Dispersion Theory
  (i) Maximize the distinctiveness of contrasts.
  (ii) Minimize articulatory effort.
  (iii) Maximize the number of contrasts.

Each of the principles is formalized as a family of rankable and violable constraints. The following are the constraints in DTC (Flemming 1995, 2004):

(2-73) Constraints in Dispersion Theory
  (i) MINDIST = *Dimension: distance*
  (ii) EFFORT MINIMIZATION, e.g. "Don't have short low vowels"
  (iii) MAXIMIZE CONTRASTS

DTC argues that phonological systems are shaped by the interaction among the above constraints.[30]

Though both DTC (Flemming 1995, 2004) and PC theory recognize contrast as a formal principle of the grammar and formulate it as a family of rankable and violable constraints, they differ on a number of points. One of the crucial differences is that while DTC evaluates phonological inventories, PC theory accounts for phonological mappings. To do so, PC theory proposes that candidates called scenarios are sets of input–output mappings. They consist of a set of inputs and related outputs. In a dispersion-theoretic approach candidates are sets of output forms (often abbreviated as inventories). This difference results in different empirical coverage of the two approaches. Dispersion Theory accounts for phonological inventories across languages and within a language. PC theory analyzes phonological processes. The empirical coverage of PC theory is illustrated in this book.

There exists a slightly modified version of DTC developed by Padgett (2003) which argues that a dispersion-theoretic approach should include standard faithfulness constraints and constraints against merging of contrasts, called *MERGE constraints. *MERGE constraints require that "no word of the output has multiple correspondents in the input" (Padgett 2003: 13). As shown by Padgett, these constraints are necessary to evaluate phonological mappings in addition to phonological inventories.[31] *MERGE constraints resemble PC_{OUT}(P) constraints in PC theory though there are differences between the two. Unlike PC constraints, *MERGE constraints of Padgett (2003) do not refer to specific phonological properties P and there is only one type of *MERGE constraint. In PC theory, there are various types of PC constraints and they refer to various phonological properties P. Also, faithfulness plays a different role in DTC (Padgett 2003) and PC theory. In PC theory, faithfulness is generalized and is placed after PC and markedness apply. In DTC, faithfulness operates together with other constraints and refers to various features (dimensions) as in standard OT. For details, see the discussion of constraints in PC theory in section 2.2. In addition, the version of DTC developed by Padgett retains (i) constraints on maximizing the distinctiveness of contrasts, called SPACEX≥1/n constraints (cf. (2-73i)), and (ii) constraints on effort minimization (cf. (2-73ii)). In this version of DTC, standard faithfulness constraints and constraints against mergers replace constraints on maximizing contrast (cf. (2-73iii)).

An important aspect of any contrast analysis is to determine what is included in the scenario and how scenarios are formed. As described in section 2.2.1, PC theory makes an important contribution in this respect by proposing a principled way to generate scenarios. In this section an algorithm is developed that shows how scenarios are formed. The issues concerning both the content and size of a scenario are addressed. This important question is also discussed in Padgett (2003) and Ní Chiosáin and Padgett (to appear).

To summarize, this chapter presented the key elements and mechanisms of PC theory. The core constraints are novel constraints on contrast. The most important implication of those constraints is that they allow for contrast transformation. This has consequences for the typology of chain shift mappings. Unlike previous approaches, it allows for push shift mappings.

In terms of constraints, PC theory recognizes that to account for phonological mappings a PC approach all the way is not sufficient. Therefore, it retains a form of input–output faithfulness in addition to PC constraints. This is different from the Dispersion Theory of Contrast (Flemming 1995, 2003; but see Padgett 2003), and further contributes to our understanding of the role and limitations of contrast in the grammar.

Notes

1. For a discussion of Kirchner's proposal see section 2.6.
2. In previous approaches, there are ways to encode morphological relatedness between forms such that forms can influence one another. In standard OT, relatedness between forms is encoded in the form of faithfulness constraints on output–output correspondence (Benua 1997, Burzio 1998), base-reduplicant identity (McCarthy and Prince 1995), optimal paradigms (McCarthy 2005), paradigm uniformity (Kenstowicz 1996, Steriade 2000) or morphological anti-faithfulness (Alderete 1999, Horwood 2001). In rule-based approaches,

relatedness between forms is encoded in underlying representations and by means of rule ordering. Yet in none of the approaches is mapping interaction stated explicitly, as it is in PC theory.

3. The term underlying form is used here to indicate the input to Gen and should not be confused with the use of this term in generative phonology.
4. This limit is to ensure that the scenarios are finite and can be adequately evaluated by the constraints. Should it turn out that there is a language where more segments are added, this limit could be revised. The actual limit is not as important as the idea that there is a limit on insertion.
5. Dispersion Theory will be discussed in section 2.7. Though PC theory evaluates sets of input–output mappings, each input–output mapping is still to be understood as telling us how to say a particular word. It only makes the assumption that you cannot determine input–output mappings in isolation.
6. Line (a) of (2-19) conflates two steps: step 1, where Gen takes an underlying form and finds all the forms that exist in the inputs of the scenarios (just by looking at its segmental length), and step 2, where Gen then builds a finite set of "output scenarios" that map the input into itself. Line (b) of (2-19) is looking at "output scenarios".
7. Double quotes in this context are used to state a constraint informally.
8. Relational PC reverses the Alternation Condition. In the Alternation Condition, if /x/ is not equal to /y/ on P, then somewhere [x] is not equal to [y] on P. But in (2-30), if [x] is not equal to [y] on P, then /x/ is not equal to /y/ on P.
9. An example of bi-directional contrasts will be provided in section 2.5.
10. Tokenized markedness makes the choice in directionality of movement for most scenarios, except the ones that contain the same number of outputs of each type; in this case generalized faithfulness makes the choice. Bi-directional scenarios are an example. See section 2.5.
11. Generalized faithfulness constraints also distinguish between chain shifts and derived environment effects (see section 2.5).
12. One can think of cases where certain phonological alternations take place in the language but some sets of segments do not undergo them.
13. In the following discussion, there will be no need for the distinction between input- and output-oriented PC nor will it be necessary to count tokens for markedness or subdivide outputs for faithfulness. This is because the following scenarios contain only two mappings. However, for continuity in the presentation of the argument, I will use all the types of constraints introduced so far. It is important to become familiar with them since they will become necessary once the scenarios get larger (see section 2.4).
14. In this example, the ranking is provable for only one PC constraint. This is expected, since the two PC constraints, input and output, both militate against neutralization, and thus if neutralization takes place, they are both violated. However, it will become clear in the following discussion that both constraints are required. It is necessary to retain both of them for an opaque scenario to ever win over other scenarios in a candidate set. If there were no input-oriented PC constraints, the so-called total merger scenario would always win over the competing chain-shift scenario (or any other competing opaque scenario for that matter). If there were no output-oriented PC constraints, the so-called transparent scenario would always win over the chain-shift scenario.
15. In reality, each scenario merges some contrasts due to ROTB (richness of the base), but the identity scenario does not merge length or rounding contrasts for the relevant inputs.
16. As reported in Karlsson (1999: 42), the observation is a bit more complex: /a/ changes to [o] in bisyllabic words if the first vowel is [a], [e], or [i] but is dropped if the first

vowel is [u] or [o]. The deletion of [a] in these contexts is probably due to OCP(labial) avoidance. It results in a chain shift mapping where shortening is combined with deletion (aa→a→Ø). Rounding or deletion also occurs in limited contexts in nouns of three or more syllables (Karlsson 1999: 42). In those words rounding or deletion cannot be a result of shortening because shortening only occurs in bisyllabic words. Interestingly, in such words, the contexts are limited to /a/ (i) preceded by a singleton [l], [n], [r], (ii) preceded by two consonants, and (iii) when the only vowel of the preceding syllable is [i]. Those cases of rounding can probably be accounted for by contextual markedness constraints that directly refer to the preceding environment, for example, *[liquid]/a. This constraint when ranked higher than conflicting PC constraints results in vowel rounding (and backing) after liquids (West 1999). Contextual markedness constraints would not account for vowel rounding in bisyllabic words because the contexts are not restricted.

17. To capture this observation formally, one could employ PC constraints that would require preservation of minimal input contrasts only. The problem with such constraints is that they would not assign violation marks to mergers of non-minimal distinctions at all (those, for example, take place in the unattested cross-corner scenario discussed in the following section). Therefore, there would be a constraint ranking under which a scenario that does not merge minimally distinct forms but incurs long-distance mergers wins. This is not a good prediction and that is why I do not pursue this approach further.
18. It is important to reiterate that contrast can only be used to explain a phonological process if a markedness constraint initiates the shift. Thus, surface true facts, like final devoicing (see section 2.3.1), are due to markedness satisfaction and not contrast. Also, PC constraints by themselves would not result in segments that are otherwise unattested in the language as long as markedness constraints against such segments outrank PC. Thanks to an anonymous reviewer for comments on this point.
19. As described in section 2.2, Gen generates more than these four inputs. But those inputs are enough to illustrate the relevant interactions.
20. It is important to point out that harmonic bounding would hold even if we included other contextual markedness constraints. Scenarios that harmonically bind one another have the same outputs and the same number of them and thus fare the same on markedness.
21. The claim here is about mapping interactions represented in (2-57) and not about the exact mappings.
22. Nasal vowels are indicated here with symbols that are commonly used in Polish literature. They reflect the orthography. In modern Polish nasalized vowels are sequences of a vowel plus nasal or a vowel plus glide depending on the environment. In Polish history, they used to be true nasal vowels (Rubach 1984).
23. Other potential cases of absolute neutralization can be found in the literature on lexical phonology (Kiparsky 1973, Rubach 1984, among others).
24. The Swedish chain shift also works this way; the fronting of back vowels would be difficult to explain as a result of markedness improvement but it has been seen as a response to overcrowding in the back. Other arguments have also been used to motivate push shifts. One of them is the temporal ordering of various changes involved in the shift (see Labov 1994).
25. If there was a separate rule for the latter process in the shift, it would be predicted that the process would occur outside of the chain shifting context. But in a push shift mapping, the latter process in the shift is always linked with the prior process, and does not apply independently.
26. Other competing scenarios are ruled out by similar means.

27. Dispersion Theory also does not admit pull shifts. Pull shifts do not improve on the distinctiveness of contrasts (and do not improve on the number of contrasts) over a comparable transparent mapping. Dispersion Theory is described in section 2.7.
28. Though not allowing for pull shifts, PC admits a sequence of changes that *resemble* a pull shift effect. Take a situation where /A/→[B] "wants to happen" (due to *A) but is blocked by /B/→[B] (to avoid neutralization). Then /B/→[C] comes along. Now the /A/→[B] map can emerge. This scenario is what I will refer to as a regular shift. It is not a pull shift because there is a *A constraint that drives /A/→[B].
29. Circular shifts *with a termination point*, for example /A/→[B], /B/→[C], /C/→[B], are predicted to occur in PC theory since the initial step in the shift improves on markedness. The tone sandhi analyzed in Barrie (2006) and Hsieh (2005) are of that form. It is important to note that such a scenario would not be harmonically bounded by /A/→[B], /B/→[B], /C/→[C] because the two scenarios differ on PC(A/B).
30. DTC has been further developed in Padgett (1997, 2003). The modifications will be described later in this section.
31. Flemming (2004) suggests that phonological mappings might be understood as relatedness among surface forms without reference to the input.

3 Phonological contrast

This chapter provides an account of stress-epenthesis interaction in Arabic dialects using the principle of contrast. Arabic dialects provide an interesting case study for the role of contrast since they differ in the way epenthesis and stress interact. To explain the differences and similarities between Arabic dialects, it is proposed that stress-epenthesis interaction is militated by a constraint on contrast. When forms with epenthetic and non-epenthetic vowels have different stress, it is argued that contrast is preserved between them despite epenthesis and is manifested as a surface stress contrast. This account is compared to several previous approaches to stress-epenthesis interaction and is found to be superior in many respects. One of the core implications of the proposal is that it predicts that the so-called onset dialects are always contrast-neutralizing, which is consistent with the facts. This chapter also discusses locality of contrast preservation.

3.1 Introduction

Epenthesis has the potential to neutralize underlying contrasts in surface forms. This takes place when identical epenthetic and non-epenthetic segments surface in the same environment and act the same with respect to phonological processes. Thus, surface words in which a given segment is present underlyingly are identical to those in which it is epenthetic. In Southern Palestinian Arabic, for example (Davis 1995, McCarthy 1997), both epenthetic and underlying *i's* block spreading of rightward [RTR] harmony. But in some cases, epenthetic and non-epenthetic words pattern differently (Alderete 1995, Archangeli 1984, 1988, Archangeli and Pulleyblank 1994, Ito 1989, Steriade 1995). In Northern Palestinian Arabic (Herzallah 1990), for example, underlying *i's* trigger de-emphaticization but epenthetic *i's* do not.

One type of contrast between words with and without epenthesis is stress assignment (Alderete 1995, 1999, Broselow 1982, Farwaneh 1995, Kager 1999a, Selkirk 1981). This chapter examines stress contrasts between epenthetic and non-epenthetic words in dialects of Arabic (Broselow 1982, Farwaneh 1995). Arabic dialects provide an interesting case for the study of stress contrasts since they vary on whether words with epenthetic and non-epenthetic vowels have the same or different stress. Dialects of Arabic can be divided into onset and coda dialects depending on the site of epenthesis (Broselow 1982, Selkirk 1981). In onset dialects, epenthesis into a tri-consonantal cluster creates an open syllable (*ka-tab-t-lu* becomes *ka-tab-ti-lu*). In coda dialects, on the other hand, epenthesis into a tri-consonantal cluster creates a closed syllable (*ki-tab-t-la* becomes *ki-ta-bit-la*). The following types of dialects will be examined:

(i) **Contrast-neutralizing dialects:** dialects in which epenthetic and non-epenthetic words have the same stress in all environments: coda dialects – Omani (Shaaban 1977), Abu Dabi (Farwaneh 1995), all onset dialects (Broselow 1992, Farwaneh 1995).
(ii) **Contrast-preserving dialects:** dialects in which epenthetic and non-epenthetic words have different stress in all environments: coda dialects – Syrian (Cowell 1964), Levantine (Farwaneh 1995, Kenstowicz 1981).
(iii) **Hybrid dialects:** dialects in which epenthetic and non-epenthetic words have different stress in word-final epenthesis but the same stress in word-medial epenthesis: coda dialect Iraqi (Broselow 1982, Erwin 1963).

Classic Optimality Theory (hereafter OT) (Prince and Smolensky 1993/2004) would not predict that all three types of dialects should exist. This is because OT is output-oriented and as an output-oriented approach to phonology, it predicts that there should be no difference in stress between epenthetic and non-epenthetic words. Words that have the same syllable structure in the output, whether epenthetic or non-epenthetic, should have the same stress. However, I will show that the proposal developed in this book predicts that all three types of dialects will exist and can be accounted for. Furthermore, unlike previous approaches to stress-epenthesis interaction, the proposal that will be developed here predicts that all onset dialects are always contrast neutralizing. (See section 3.7 for a comparison with previous approaches.)

The main observation in this chapter is that when epenthetic and non-epenthetic words have different stress, the underlying contrast between them is preserved on the surface despite epenthesis and is realized as surface stress contrast. In other words, the underlying segmental contrast in the presence versus absence of a vowel is manifested as surface contrast in prosodic prominence. Conversely, when epenthetic and non-epenthetic words have the same stress, the underlying contrast between them is neutralized. This observation will be implemented using the framework of PC theory (see Chapter 2).

This chapter contributes to the growing body of work on the status of contrast in phonology and examines the application of contrast principles to stress-epenthesis interaction (see references in Chapter 1).

Previous approaches to stress-epenthesis interaction in OT include positional faithfulness (Alderete 1995, 1999, Kager 1999a, Revithiadou 1999), LPM-OT (Kiparsky 2000, 2002), sympathy theory (McCarthy 1999), output–output correspondence (Benua 1997, Kager 1999a, 1999b), turbidity (Goldrick and Smolensky 1999), local conjunction (Kirchner 1996, Łubowicz 2002, Smolensky 1993, 1997), targeted constraints (Wilson 2001), comparative markedness (McCarthy 2003b), and the theory of chains (McCarthy 2007). In this work, I propose an account in terms of preserving contrast and argue that it makes superior predictions to previous approaches.

This chapter is organized as follows. Section 3.2 describes the problem and gives an overview of the analysis. Section 3.3 presents the framework. Section 3.4 applies the proposal to Arabic. Section 3.5 discusses predictions of the proposal. Section 3.6 addresses the issue of locality of contrast preservation. Section 3.7 compares the proposal to previous approaches to stress-epenthesis interaction. Finally, section 3.8 is the conclusion.

3.2 Proposal overview

One of the cases that will be analyzed in this chapter is a contrast-preserving dialect, Syrian. In Syrian (Cowell 1964), epenthetic and non-epenthetic words have different stress. Syrian and other dialects that will be analyzed here have Latin stress. In Latin, the penult is stressed if the syllable is heavy, otherwise the antepenult is stressed. Final syllables are not stressed, except in monosyllables. Heavy syllables consist of a syllable with a long vowel or a closed syllable.

Latin stress is described as a moraic trochee system with final syllable extrametricality (Apoussidou and Boersma 2004, Hayes 1995, Jacobs 2000, Mester 1994, Prince and Smolensky 1993/2004). Moraic trochees consist of two light syllables with initial prominence or a single heavy syllable. Feet are assigned right to left and main stress falls on the rightmost foot in the prosodic word.

As shown below, in Syrian, non-epenthetic words with a closed penult have penultimate stress, as expected (see (3-1)). This is a moraic trochee system and stress falls on the heavy penult. Epenthetic words with a closed penult, however, have unexpected antepenultimate stress. Instead of stress falling on the closed penultimate syllable, it falls on the antepenult (see (3-2)). Epenthetic vowels are in bold font. The examples are from Cowell (1964).[1]

(3-1) Non-epenthetic words – penultimate stress

	Example	Gloss	Reference	Footing
a.	Da(ráb)ha	'he hit her'	C 20	L(H)<L>
b.	sak(kə́r)ha	'close it (fem.)'	C 20	H(H)<L>
c.	ʔa(kál)tu	'you (pl.) ate'	C 173	L(H)<L>
d.	tɛ(nə́s)kon	'your (pl.) tennis'	pc	L(H)<H>

(3-2) Epenthetic words – antepenultimate stress

	Example	Gloss	Reference	Footing
a.	(ʔát**ə**l)na	'the killing of us'	pc	*ʔa(t**ə́**l)na
b.	(ʔák**ə**l)ton	'their meal'	pc	*ʔa(k**ə́**l)ton
c.	(náz**ə**l)ti	'my descent'	pc	*na(z**ə́**l)ti
d.	(ʔə́b**ə**n)kon	'your (pl.) son'	C 32	*ʔə(b**ə́**n)kon

The question is why there exists a difference in stress between identical epenthetic and non-epenthetic words. As will be explained below, the words are identical in the properties relevant for stress assignment and not necessarily in segmental content.

In standard OT, there should be no difference in stress between epenthetic and non-epenthetic forms with identical syllable structure in the output. OT is output-oriented and since stress is assigned based on the output form, the forms in (3-1) and (3-2) should have the same stress.

Given Latin stress, we expect forms in (3-2) to have penultimate stress (stressing a heavy penult), predicting unattested **ʔa(tə́l)na* and not the actual *(ʔátəl)na*. In these forms, the penultimate syllable is closed and thus should count as heavy. As a heavy syllable, we expect it to bear stress.

The key proposal here is that the difference in stress between epenthetic and non-epenthetic words signals an underlying distinction in the presence versus absence of a vowel that would otherwise be lost in the output due to epenthesis. Thus, when words with and without epenthesis have different stress, the underlying contrast between them is preserved on the surface and manifested as a surface stress contrast, non-epenthetic *tɛ(nə́s)kon* (see (3-1d)) versus epenthetic *(ʔə́bən)kon* (see (3-2d)) .

To explain why stress falls on the antepenultimate syllable in epenthetic words in (3-2), I will propose that the syllable with an epenthetic vowel counts as a light syllable. As has been proposed in the literature, coda consonants in Arabic are moraic and thus closed syllables count as heavy for purposes of stress assignment and other metrical processes (see Farwaneh 1995, Hayes 1989, 1995, McCarthy and Prince 1990a, 1990b). However, I observe that in contrast-preserving dialects such as Syrian closed epenthetic syllables count as light for purposes of stress assignment (Piggott 1995). Given the forms in (3-2), the epenthetic syllable *bən* in *(ʔə́.bən).kon* counts as light instead of heavy and so stress is assigned to the antepenultimate syllable. This results in a well-formed moraic trochee that consists of two light syllables. To explain why epenthetic closed syllables count as light, I will propose that coda consonants of epenthetic syllables are non-moraic. This leads to a different foot structure of an epenthetic word, and thus different stress. For a more in depth discussion of the relation between moraic representation and heavy/light syllables, see Hayes (1995).

Formally, as explained in the following sections, it will be proposed that in contrast-preserving dialects the need to preserve contrast between epenthetic and non-epenthetic forms compels the non-moraic coda consonant of the epenthetic syllable. In other words, the need to preserve contrast can alter the weight system of the language and thus change stress. The account here joins the observations that contrast is preserved in Syrian between epenthetic and non-epenthetic words and that closed epenthetic syllables count as light instead of heavy.[2]

This proposal will be implemented in PC theory. There have been numerous approaches to address this problem in OT but, as will be argued in section 3.7, none are as successful as the contrast account. The next section reviews the framework.

3.3 PC theory review

The proposal will be implemented in the framework of PC theory. The basic architecture of PC theory has been described in Chapter 2 using the example of chain shift mappings. In what follows, I will discuss the elements of the framework that are essential for the analysis of Arabic.

3.3.1 Constraints on contrast

As we have seen in Chapter 2, the core of PC theory is that contrast exists as an imperative in the grammar which in the framework of OT can be formulated as a family of rankable and violable constraints on preserving contrasts, called PC constraints. Constraints on contrast demand that pairs of words that contrast in the input in a given phonological property P, contrast on the surface but not necessarily in the same property P (see section 2.2.2.1). The relevant definitions are recalled below.

(3-3) $PC_{IN}(P)$
"If inputs are distinct in P, they need to remain distinct in the output (not necessarily in P)."
Formally, assign one mark for every pair of inputs, in_a and in_b, if in_a has P and in_b lacks P, $in_a \rightarrow out_k$, and $in_b \rightarrow out_k$.

(3-4) Definition of contrast in P
A pair of inputs, in_a and in_b, contrast in P when corresponding segments in those inputs, seg_a and seg_b, are such that seg_a has P and seg_b lacks P.[3]

The key property of PC constraints is that, unlike standard faithfulness, they admit cases where a given contrast is expressed on the surface in a different way than in the underlying form, called *contrast transformation.* In Arabic, the contrast in the presence versus absence of a vowel is manifested as surface contrast in stress.

As described in Chapter 2, constraints on contrast interact with each other and with conflicting markedness constraints. This interaction takes place in stage 1 of Eval. But not all patterns of contrast preservation can be distinguished by the interaction of contrast and markedness. To evaluate contrast effectively, there are generalized faithfulness constraints in the theory in stage 2 of Eval. In cases of contrast displacement, as in Arabic, generalized faithfulness constraints are formulated as constraints on recoverability. Recoverability constraints will be introduced in section 3.4.1. They will be used both in the current chapter and Chapter 4.

3.3.2 The candidate

As shown in Chapter 2, to evaluate constraints on contrast, we need to evaluate pairs of input–output mappings rather than individual mappings as in standard OT. The contrast candidate is referred to as a scenario (cf. Flemming 1995, 1996, Padgett 1997, 2000). In a contrast-preserving scenario, shown in (3-5), non-epenthetic and epenthetic words have different stress. The non-epenthetic form has penultimate stress while the epenthetic form has antepenultimate stress. In a contrast-neutralizing scenario, on the other hand, shown in (3-6), non-epenthetic and epenthetic words have the same stress. Both non-epenthetic and epenthetic forms have penultimate stress. In the scenarios below, the epenthetic vowel is in bold font.

(3-5) Contrast-preserving scenario

Non-epenthetic	/CVCVC-CV/	→	cv(cv́c$_{\mu}$)cv	L(H)L	penultimate stress
Epenthetic	/CVC∅C-CV/	→	(cv́c**v**c)cv	(L**L**)L	antepenultimate stress

(3-6) Contrast-neutralizing scenario

Non-epenthetic	/CVCVC-CV/	→	cv(cv́c$_{\mu}$)cv	L(H)L	penultimate stress
Epenthetic	/CVC∅C-CV/	→	cv(c**v́**c$_{\mu}$)cv	L(**H**)L	penultimate stress

The locus of epenthesis in the input is marked with a null sign. In this framework, contrast is evaluated over the set of possible words of the language and not the actual words. When evaluating contrasts in stress and epenthesis, what matters is that forms in a scenario are identical in syllable structure and epenthesis but not necessarily in segmental content. For example, the actual words *tɛ(nə́s)kon* without epenthesis and *(ʔə́bən)kon* with epenthesis have the same syllable structure in the output but different segmental content, while hypothetical *ʔə(bə́n)kon* without epenthesis and actual *(ʔə́bən)kon* with epenthesis have the same syllable structure and segmental content. Both forms are part of the same scenario under PC theory because the syllable structure is the same. Thus, for ease of presentation I will be using the CV (consonant-vowel) notation. Light syllables are marked with L, while heavy syllables are marked with H. Stressed syllables are marked with an accent.[4]

Since this chapter discusses a contrast in presence vs. absence of a vowel, I will follow Wolf and McCarthy (2009) in their proposal to evaluate inputs and outputs as strings rather than individual segments. Under their proposal, epenthesis is represented directly in the input. In this chapter, there are zero symbols included in the inputs for epenthetic cases. If inputs and outputs were evaluated as segments rather than strings, epenthesis would not be directly marked in the input. Epenthetic inputs would simply contain fewer segments than corresponding outputs. This assumption becomes relevant in section 3.6 in the formulation of locality.

Scenarios in a candidate set represent various mapping coexistence patterns (see section 2.2.1). The optimal scenario is chosen by the interaction among constraints. PC constraints interact with each other and with markedness constraints, resulting in preservation or neutralization of underlying distinctions in surface forms.

3.3.3 The constraints in Arabic

The relevant PC constraint in Arabic demands that inputs that contrast in the presence versus absence of a vowel – epenthetic and non-epenthetic forms – contrast in the output in some way. The relevant constraint is defined in (3-7).

(3-7) $PC_{IN}(V/\varnothing)$
"If inputs are distinct in the presence/absence of a vowel, they need to remain distinct in the output (not necessarily in V/∅)."

Formally, assign one mark for every pair of inputs, in_a and in_b, if in_a has V and in_b lacks V, $in_a \rightarrow out_k$, and $in_b \rightarrow out_k$.

This constraint is satisfied when epenthetic and non-epenthetic words have different stress in the output despite epenthesis. In Arabic, the input contrast in presence vs. absence of a vowel is preserved in the output by a different stress due to the difference in the moraic representation of the coda consonant of the epenthetic syllable (see 3.4.1). The $PC_{IN}(V/\varnothing)$ constraint evaluates a difference in stress between the outputs (an audible contrast) which comes about by a difference in moraicity (a structural or representational property). The PC constraint would be satisfied if two outputs had a different moraic structure but the same stress.[5]

Stress is a good choice to preserve contrast. Stress is predictable in Arabic, and thus input stress contrasts neutralize on the actual stress pattern in the output under the compulsion of constraints on stress placement.

Furthermore, I propose that the need to preserve contrast can alter the weight system of the language and consequently change stress. Formally, the constraint on contrast defined in (3-7) can compel a violation of the relevant markedness constraint that assigns a mora to a coda consonant. The relevant markedness constraint is given below:

(3-8) Weight-By-Position (WBP) (Gordon 2002, Hayes 1989, 1995, Morén 2001, Rosenthall and van der Hulst 1999)
A coda consonant must bear a mora, and this mora belongs exclusively to this consonant (i.e. it is not shared with a vowel).[6]

Dialects will differ in the relative rankings of these constraints. Since WBP is a violable constraint both contrast-preserving and contrast-neutralizing dialects are possible.

The difference in the moraic structure between syllables with epenthetic and non-epenthetic vowels was previously proposed in the literature by Piggott (1995). For a discussion of Piggott's account see section 3.7.

3.4 The analysis

This section applies the PC proposal to Arabic. I first discuss a contrast-preserving dialect – Syrian, followed by a contrast-neutralizing dialect – Omani, and a hybrid dialect – Iraqi. All dialects discussed in this section have Latin type stress, as described in section 3.2.

3.4.1 Contrast preservation

In Syrian (Cowell 1964), there is a process of schwa epenthesis. Epenthesis breaks up consonant clusters (e.g. *l+ktāb → ləktāb* 'the book', *ʔakl → ʔakəl* 'food'). Since there are other sources of schwa in the same environment, epenthesis is able to merge the underlying contrast between epenthetic and non-epenthetic words. Epenthetic and non-epenthetic schwas are pronounced the same (see Cowell 1964: 19–33). This data has also been verified by a native speaker of Syrian.

In Syrian, epenthetic and non-epenthetic words have different stress. Let us begin with medial epenthesis. Non-epenthetic words stress a heavy penult (see (3-9)). But when a heavy penult is formed by epenthesis, stress falls on the antepenultimate syllable and not, as expected, the penultimate syllable (see (3-10)).

(3-9) Non-epenthetic words – penultimate stress

Example	**Gloss**	**Reference**	**Underlying**
a. Da(ráb)ha	'he hit her'	C 20	/Darab-ha/
b. sak(kə́r)ha	'close it' (fem.)	C 20	/sakkər-ha/
c. ʔa(kál)tu	'you (pl.) ate'	C 173	/ʔakal-t-u/
d. ʔən(Sə́l)na	'our consul'	C 28	/ʔənSol-na/
e. tɛ(nə́s)kon	'your (pl.) tennis'	pc	/tɛnas-kon/

(3-10) Medial epenthesis – antepenultimate stress

Example	**Gloss**	**Reference**	**Underlying**	**Footing**
f. (ʔákəl)ton	'their meal'	pc	/ʔakl(t)-on/	*ʔa(kə́l)ton
g. (názəl)ti	'my descent'	pc	/nazl(t)-i/	*na(zə́l)ti
h. (ʔátəl)na	'the killing of us'	pc	/ʔatl-na/	*ʔa(tə́l)na
i. (ʔə́bən)kon	'your (pl.) son'	C 32	/ʔəbn-kon/	*ʔə(bə́n)kon

Similarly, when there is no heavy penult, stress falls on the antepenultimate syllable in non-epenthetic words (see (3-11)). But words with final epenthesis and a light penult have penultimate stress and not, as expected, antepenultimate (see (3-12)).

(3-11) Non-epenthetic words – antepenultimate stress

Example	**Gloss**	**Reference**	**Underlying**
a. (lə́Hi)tak	'your (masc.) beard'	C 166	/lə́Hye(t)-ak/
b. (máši)tak	'your (masc.) walk'	pc	/mašye(t)-ak/
c. (fáta)Het	'she opened'	C 197	/fataH-et/
d. (nkása)ret	'it (fem.) was broken'	C 198	/nkasar-et/

(3-12) Final epenthesis - penultimate stress

Example	**Gloss**	**Reference**	**Underlying**	**Footing**
a. sa(dáʔət)	'I told the truth'	C 16	/sadaʔ-t/	*(sáda)ʔət
b. ʔa(kálət)	'I ate'	pc	/ʔakal-t/	*(ʔáka)lət
c. ka(tábət)	'I wrote'	C 55	/katab-t/	*(káta)bət

The stress pattern of epenthetic and non-epenthetic words in Syrian is represented schematically below. In case of epenthesis into the penult, referred to as medial epenthesis, stress is penultimate in non-epenthetic words but antepenultimate in epenthetic words. Similarly, in case of epenthesis into the final syllable, referred to as final epenthesis, stress in non-epenthetic words is antepenultimate but in epenthetic words stress is penultimate.

(3-13) Medial epenthesis – contrast is preserved

Non-epenthetic	/CVCVC-CV/	→	cv(cv́c_μ)cv	penultimate stress
Epenthetic	/CVC∅C-CV/	→	(cv́cəc)cv	antepenultimate stress

(3-14) Final epenthesis – contrast is preserved

Non-epenthetic	/CVCVC-VC/	→	(cv́cv)cvc_μ	antepenultimate stress
Epenthetic	/CVCVC-∅C/	→	cv(cv́cəc)	penultimate stress

As described in section 3.3, the proposal here is that epenthetic and non-epenthetic words in Syrian contrast on the surface by different stress. In the proposal developed in this chapter, coda consonants of epenthetic syllables are non-moraic. This results in a different foot structure and thus, different stress. Formally, a constraint on preserving contrast between epenthetic and non-epenthetic words, PC_{IN}(V/∅), outranks the markedness constraint that assigns a mora to the coda consonant, WBP, compelling a moraless coda consonant in the epenthetic syllable. In effect, the underlying contrast in the presence versus absence of a vowel is manifested as surface contrast in prosodic prominence.

The following tableaux illustrate the analysis. I consider both medial and final epenthesis. In each case, a contrast-preserving scenario is compared to a contrast-neutralizing scenario. In both cases the scenario with different stress for epenthetic and non-epenthetic words, the contrast-preserving scenario, scenario (i), wins.

(3-15) Medial epenthesis

Scenarios		PC_{IN}(V/∅)	WBP
(i) Contrast is preserved ☞	/CVC∅C-CV/ → (cv́cvc)cv /CVCVC-CV/ → cv(cv́c_μ)cv		*
(ii) Contrast is neutralized	/CVC∅C-CV/ → cv(cv́c_μ)cv /CVCVC-CV/ → cv(cv́c_μ)cv	*!	

(3-16) Final epenthesis

Scenarios		PC_{IN}(V/∅)	WBP
(i) Contrast is preserved ☞	/CVCVC-∅C/ → cv(cv́cvc) /CVCVC-VC/ → (cv́cv)cvc_μ		*
(ii) Contrast is neutralized	/CVCVC-∅C/ → (cv́cv)cvc_μ /CVCVC-VC/ → (cv́cv)cvc_μ	*!	

Scenario (i) is chosen as optimal since it preserves the contrast between epenthetic and non-epenthetic words. Epenthetic and non-epenthetic words have different stress and thus contrast is maintained between them despite epenthesis.

In addition, in the case of final epenthesis, I have assumed here that the foot is final in the prosodic word. Thus, *FINALFOOT, which bans a final foot in a PrWd, must be ranked below the constraint on contrast, PC_{IN}(V/∅).

(3-17) The ranking of *FINALFOOT

Scenarios		PC_{IN} (V/∅)	WBP	*FINAL FOOT
(i) Contrast is preserved ☞	/CVCVC-∅C/ → cv(cv́cvc) /CVCVC-VC/ → (cv́cv)cvc_μ		*	*
(ii) Contrast is neutralized	/CVCVC-∅C/ → (cv́cv)cvc_μ /CVCVC-VC/ → (cv́cv)cvc_μ	*!		

The candidate with a final foot wins since it preserves contrast.[7]

There are, of course, other imaginable prosodic analyses of these forms. But none are as effective as (3-15)–(3-17) when the full analysis is considered. First, in the case of final epenthesis, I have assumed that the foot is final in the prosodic word. One alternative would be to assume that the final consonant in *kitábit* constitutes its own syllable outside of the main stressed foot. We would then have footing as in *ki.(tá.bi.)t* with the final consonant unparsed. However, if *t* constituted its own syllable, then there would be no cluster within a syllable to be broken up by the epenthetic vowel and thus epenthesis would not be motivated.

I have also crucially assumed that feet are well-formed at the expense of weight, and not the other way around. That is, we always strive to have a licit moraic trochee. To do so, the weight of the epenthetic syllable is altered so that it is a light syllable. An alternative would be to assume that syllable weight is obeyed but feet are degenerate. Following Broselow (1992), I assume that in Arabic FOOTBINARITY is undominated. Evidence comes from a strict minimal word requirement by which words have to be minimally bimoraic. Therefore, I do not adopt the monomoraic foot alternative. This is illustrated below.

(3-18) No degenerate feet

Scenarios		FTBINARITY	PC_{IN}(V/∅)	WBP
(i) Contrast is preserved ☞	/CVC∅C-CV/ → (cv́cvc)cv /CVCVC-CV/ → cv(cv́c_μ)cv			*
(ii) Contrast is neutralized	/CVC∅C-CV/ → cv(cv́c_μ)cv /CVCVC-CV/ → cv(cv́c_μ)cv		*!	
(iii) Alternative (monomoraic foot)	/CVC∅C-CV/ → (cv́)cv$c_\mu$cv /CVCVC-CV/ → cv(cv́c_μ)cv	*!		

Additional evidence in favor of limiting the weight of epenthetic syllables and against the degenerate foot alternative comes from the typological predictions this proposal makes with respect to onset dialects (section 3.5) and hybrid cases as in Iraqi Arabic (section 3.4.3).

In addition to the constraints on contrast and markedness (weight requirements), there are also constraints on recoverability which resolve ties between scenarios that are otherwise identical on contrast and markedness. Constraints on recoverability belong to stage 2 of Eval.

(3-19) RECOVER (P)

Let a pair of inputs in_a and in_b minimally contrast in P and corresponding outputs minimally contrast in P', if in_a has P and in_b lacks P, then out_a has P′ and out_b lacks P′.

"The minimal input contrast in P needs to be preserved in the output in the same direction."

Constraints on recoverability select a scenario in which outputs are more similar to their inputs. In terms of contrasts, they select a scenario in which an output contrast is manifested in the same direction as in the input. They choose a scenario which is "more recoverable" – the input contrast can be read off from the distribution of the corresponding contrast in the output. The two properties referred to in the recoverability constraints are determined in stage 1 of Eval. The "directionality" depends on our assumptions about how phonological properties are represented in the theory.

Constraints on recoverability resemble MAX(feature) constraints where the relevant feature is preserved from the input in the output but displaced from its original position (Lombardi 2001). The main difference between the MAX(feature) approach and RECOVER(P) constraints is that MAX(feature) is satisfied only when inputs and corresponding outputs contain identical features while recoverability is satisfied by forms where input and output contrasts are not necessarily identical. Unlike MAX(feature), recoverability allows for contrast transformation.

In Arabic:

(3-20) RECOVER (V/∅)

Let a pair of inputs in_a and in_b minimally contrast in V/∅ and corresponding outputs minimally contrast in μ/∅, if in_a has V and in_b lacks V, then out_a has μ and out_b lacks μ (μ=mora).

The constraint in (3-20) chooses a scenario in which the output moraless coda is in the mapping that lacks the vowel in the input. Consequently, this is the mapping that has irregular stress. It rules out a scenario in which it is the mapping with an underlying vowel that gets irregular stress while the mapping with an epenthetic vowel has regular stress, the so-called permuted scenario.

(3-21) Contrast-preserving scenario

Non-epenthetic	/CVCVC-CV/ →	cv(cv́$c_μ$)cv	L(<u>H</u>)L	penultimate stress
Epenthetic	/CVC∅C-CV/ →	(cv́cvc)cv	(<u>L</u>L)L	antepenultimate stress

(3-22) Permuted scenario

Non-epenthetic	/CVCVC-CV/ →	(cv́cvc)cv	(<u>L</u>L)L	antepenultimate stress
Epenthetic	/CVC∅C-CV/ →	cv(cv́c_{μ})cv	L(<u>H</u>)L	penultimate stress

(3-23) Permuted scenario – harmonically bounded

Scenarios		PC_{IN}(V/∅)	WBP	RECOVER (V/∅)
(i) Contrast preserving ☞	/CVC∅C-CV/ → (cv́cvc)cv /CVCVC-CV/ → cv(cv́c_{μ})cv		*	
(ii) Permuted scenario	/CVC∅C-CV/ → cv(cv́c_{μ})cv /CVCVC-CV/ → (cv́cvc)cv		*	*!

It is important to note that the permuted scenario is harmonically bounded on the recoverability constraint and thus, will never come out as optimal. As far as I know, this is consistent with the facts. I am not aware of any language where it is the mapping with an epenthetic vowel that gets regular stress while the underlying mapping has irregular stress.

3.4.2 Contrast neutralization

Consider now the Omani dialect, where epenthetic and non-epenthetic words have the same stress. In Omani (Farwaneh 1995, Qafisheh 1977, Shaaban 1977), the high vowel [i] is epenthesized to improve syllabification (e.g., /gism/ → gis**i**m 'body', /ʔakl+hum/ → ʔak**i**l+hum 'their (masc.) food').

Unlike Syrian, in Omani, speakers do not differentiate words with epenthetic and non-epenthetic vowels. Epenthetic and non-epenthetic words have the same stress in all environments. The dialect analyzed in this section has Latin stress. The data comes from Farwaneh (1995), Qafisheh (1977), and Shaaban (1977), and is confirmed by a native speaker. The dialect analyzed in this section is spoken in the capital of Oman.[8]

In case of a heavy penult, stress is penultimate regardless of whether the penult is present in the input or created by epenthesis:

(3-24) Non-epenthetic words – penultimate stress

Example	Gloss	Reference	Underlying
a. wa(lád)hum	'their (masc.) son'	Q 32	/walad-hum/
b. si(máč)ha	'her fish'	Q 167	/simač-ha/
c. ma(lík)ne	'our King'	S 66	/malik-na/

(3-25) Medial epenthesis – penultimate stress

Example	Gloss	Reference	Underlying
a. ʔa(kíl)hum	'their (masc.) food'	F 138	/ʔakl-hum/
b. qa(bír)he	'her grave'	F 138	/qabr-ha/
c. ha(ðín)kum	'your (pl.) embrace'	F 138	/haðn-kum/

The same is true when epenthesis occurs in the final syllable. In final epenthesis, stress is the same in both epenthetic and non-epenthetic forms. The following data is novel and elicited from a native speaker of Omani.[9]

(3-26) Non epenthetic words – antepenultimate stress

Example	Gloss	Reference	Underlying
a. (mán).zi.la	'status'	F 137	/manzila/
b. (már).ka.bak	'your (masc.) boat'	F 137	/markab-ak/
c. (mís).gi.dak	'your (masc.) mosque'	F 137	/misgid-ak/

(3-27) Final epenthesis – Antepenultimate stress

Example	Gloss	Reference	Underlying
a. sa.(ráq).la.ħin	'he stole a tune'	pc	/saraq # laħn/
b. sa.(ráq).sa.ħib	'he stole a friend'	pc	/saraq # saħib/
c. da.(ráz).ga.bir	'he studied algebra'	pc	/daras # gabr/
d. da.(rás).ma.lik	'he studied the king'	pc	/daras # malik/

This is represented schematically below. In both medial and final epenthesis, epenthetic and non-epenthetic words are stressed the same.

(3-28) Medial epenthesis – contrast is neutralized

Non epenthetic	/CVCVC-CVC/	→	cv(cv́c$_{\mu}$)cvc$_{\mu}$	penultimate stress
Epenthetic	/CVC∅C-CVC/	→	cv(cv́c$_{\mu}$)cvc$_{\mu}$	penultimate stress

(3-29) Final epenthesis - contrast is neutralized

Non-epenthetic	/CVCVC-CVCVC/	→	cv(cv́c$_{\mu}$)cvcvc$_{\mu}$	antepenultimate stress
Epenthetic	/CVCVC-CVC∅C/	→	cv(cv́c$_{\mu}$)cvcvc$_{\mu}$	antepenultimate stress

Under the proposal here, in a contrast-neutralizing dialect, it is more important to obey syllable weight than it is to preserve contrast. Formally, it is more important to satisfy WBP than to satisfy PC. Thus, both in medial and final epenthesis stress is assigned as expected. The winning candidate assigns a mora to the coda consonant in accordance with WBP and epenthetic and non-epenthetic words have the same stress. Tableaux (3-30) and (3-31) illustrate medial and final epenthesis.

(3-30) Medial epenthesis

Scenarios		WBP	PC$_{IN}$(V/∅)
(i) Contrast is preserved	/CVC∅C-CV/ → (cv́cvc)cv /CVCVC-CV/ → cv(cv́c$_{\mu}$)cv	*!	
(ii) Contrast is neutralized ☞	/CVC∅C-CV/ → cv(cv́c$_{\mu}$)cv /CVCVC-CV/ → cv(cv́c$_{\mu}$)cv		*

(3-31) Final epenthesis

Scenarios		WBP	PC$_{IN}$(V/∅)
(i) Contrast is preserved	/CVCVC-CVC∅C/ → cvcvc$_{\mu}$(cv́cvc) /CVCVC-CVCVC/ → cv(cv́c$_{\mu}$)cvcvc$_{\mu}$	*!	
(ii) Contrast is neutralized ☞	/CVCVC-CVC∅C/ → cv(cv́c$_{\mu}$)cvcvc$_{\mu}$ /CVCVC-CVCVC/ → cv(cv́c$_{\mu}$)cvcvc$_{\mu}$		*

In both instances, the contrast-neutralizing scenario wins since it satisfies WBP. Thus, epenthetic and non-epenthetic forms have the same stress.

So far, I have analyzed a contrast-preserving dialect and a contrast-neutralizing dialect. The core difference between the two lies in the relative ranking of WBP and PC.

3.4.3 Hybrid dialect

We now turn to a dialect where contrast is preserved but only in some positions. In Iraqi Arabic (Broselow 1982, Erwin 1963) epenthesis is contrast preserving but only word-finally. That is, epenthetic and non-epenthetic words have the same stress in word-medial epenthesis (see (3-32)–(3-33)) but they contrast in word-final epenthesis (see (3-34)–(3-35)).

Consider first the stress pattern of non-epenthetic words with a heavy penult and words where the heavy penult is formed by epenthesis. In both instances, stress is penultimate.[10]

(3-32) Non-epenthetic words – penultimate stress

Example	Gloss	Reference	Underlying
a. sal(lát)ha	'her basket'	E 41	/salla(t)-ha/
b. ga(lám)ha	'her pencil'	E 276	/galam-ha/
c. gah(wát)ha	'we proved'	E 276	/gahwa(t)-ha/

(3-33) Medial epenthesis – penultimate stress

Example	Gloss	Reference	Underlying
a. ʔi(bín)ha	'her son'	E 41	/ʔibn-ha/
b. gi(lít)la	'I told him'	F 16	/gil-t-la/
c. ʔu(xút)ha	'her sister'	F 276	/ʔuxt-ha/

The situation is different in final epenthesis. In final epenthesis, epenthetic words have penultimate stress while identical non-epenthetic words have antepenultimate stress.

(3-34) Final epenthesis – penultimate stress

Example	Gloss	Reference	Underlying
a. ki(tábi**t**)	'I wrote'	E 87	/kitab-t/
b. ʔa(káli**t**)	'I ate'	E 88	/ʔakal-t/
c. xaa(bári**t**)	'I phoned'	E 89	/xaabar-t/
d. tar(jámi**t**)	'I translated'	E 42	/tarjam-t/

(3-35) Non-epenthetic words – antepenultimate stress

Example	Gloss	Reference	Underlying
a. (ʔára)dan	'never'	E 313	/ʔabad-an/
b. (mád)rasa	'school'	E 41	/madrasa/
c. (šári)ka	'company'	E 41	/šarika/

In my proposal the V/∅ contrast is preserved on the surface by creating a mora-less coda, which affects the foot structure of a word and, consequently, main-stress placement. Since in Iraqi contrast is preserved word-finally but not word-medially, we need to explain why a mora-less coda is permitted word-finally but banned from a word-medial position.[11]

It has been observed that prosodic constituents (e.g. segments, syllables, and feet) at the periphery of a prosodic or a morphological domain (e.g. prosodic word, stem, and phrase) have special status. They can be deficient in structure or different in affiliation from identical constituents trapped within a string. This special property of edge-most constituents is captured in the theories of incomplete syllabification (McCarthy and Prince 1990a, 1990b), extrametricality (Hayes 1982, 1995, Kager 1995, Liberman and Prince 1977), extrasyllabicity (Rubach and Booij 1990), typological observations on codas restricted to word-final positions (McCarthy 1993, Piggott 1999), and the representation of contour segments (Piggott 1988). McCarthy and Prince (1990a, 1990b), for example, propose that edge-most consonants in Arabic, unlike medial consonants, can form incomplete syllables. Rubach (1996) and Rubach and Booij (1990) observe that, in Polish, word-initial extrasyllabic consonants behave differently from non-initial consonants with respect to segmental processes, for example final devoicing, voice assimilation, degemination. They capture this difference formally by proposing separate PrWd-adjunction processes for word-initial versus non-word-initial consonants. Since the two adjunctions can occur at different stages of the derivation, segments are predicted to behave differently with respect to segmental processes depending on their position in a PrWd. For other accounts of extrasyllabicity, see Halle and Vergnaud (1987), Ito (1982), and Borowsky (1986).

To capture this observation, I propose a markedness constraint called Mora-Contiguity that does not allow word-medial moraless codas. As will be explained below, I will assume, following previous work, that a prosodic word has a contiguous moraic structure, and moraless consonants word-medially disrupt contiguity at the level of moras. Like other OT constraints, MORA-CONTIGUITY is a violable constraint and thus moraless codas are permitted word-medially when compelled by higher-ranked constraints.[12]

Following Hyman (1985), Ito (1989), and Zec (1988), I assume that in weight-sensitive languages each segment of a syllable bears a mora. Onsets share a mora with the following vowel. Thus, a CVC syllable in a weight-sensitive language has the following moraic structure:

(3-36) Moraic representation

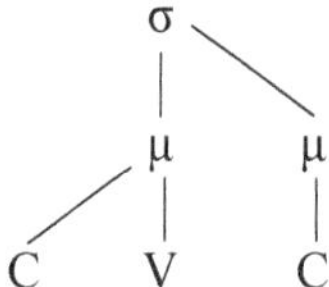

This structure finds motivation in tonal processes (Hyman 1985), language games where onsets act as constituents (Katada 1990), and in the theory of epenthesis (Ito 1989). See also Broselow *et al.* (1997).

Assuming the above syllable structure, MORA-CONTIGUITY is defined as follows:

(3-37) Definition of MORA-CONTIGUITY
In αβδ, if α∈μ and δ∈μ, then β∈μ,
where αβδ = segments, and μ = the set of segments associated with μ (moras).

Informally, this constraint enforces moraic contiguity over contiguous strings of segments. It is violated whenever contiguity is disrupted, as illustrated below:

(3-38) Violation of MORA-CONTIGUITY

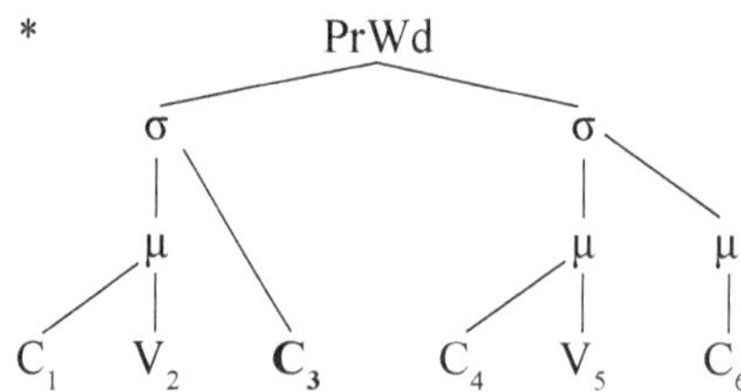

In (3-38), there is a moraless coda, C_3, medially in the string of segments, and so contiguity is disrupted. MORA-CONTIGUITY is a markedness constraint with no reference to the input. For contiguity as a faithfulness constraint, see McCarthy and Prince (1995), among others. In PC theory, there are no standard faithfulness constraints. As discussed, the inventory of constraints includes markedness and contrast in stage 1 of Eval aided by generalized faithfulness and recoverability in stage 2 of Eval.[13]

There are various possible representations of a moraless coda (Hayes 1989, McCarthy and Prince 1996, Sherer 1994, Zec 1988). As discussed in Sherer (1994), according to prosodic licensing (Ito 1988), there are various positions to which a moraless coda consonant can be adjoined. In addition to the representation shown above where the moraless coda consonant is adjoined directly to the syllable node, other representations include the moraless coda consonant adjoined to the mora of the preceding vowel, to the foot or PrWd (Rubach and Booij 1990). Such a consonant could also form a degenerate syllable (McCarthy and Prince 1990a, 1990b). Though certain alternatives make clear empirical predictions, as discussed in Sherer (1994), it is difficult to distinguish between the alternatives of having the moraless coda consonant adjoined directly to the syllable node (as above) or to the mora of the preceding vowel. Both representations seem to make the same predictions in most cases (Sherer 1994). In the account of hybrid dialects, I have assumed a representation where the moraless coda consonant is directly adjoined to the syllable node and formulated mora-contiguity accordingly. [14]

I propose that contrast is preserved in Iraqi Arabic (PC_{IN}(V/∅) >>WBP) unless it would incur a violation of MORA-CONTIGUITY. Thus, MORA-CONTIGUITY outranks PC_{IN}(V/∅). As a result, the weight of a medial syllable with an epenthetic vowel cannot be altered to preserve contrast and so word-medial epenthesis is non-contrast-preserving:

(3-39) Hybrid ranking
MORA-CONTIGUITY >> PC_{IN}(V/∅) >> WBP

This is illustrated in the following tableau:

(3-40) Medial epenthesis – contrast is neutralized

Scenarios		MORA CONTIGUITY	PC_{IN} (V/∅)	WBP
(i) Non-moraic coda	/CVC∅C CV/ → (cvcvc)cv /CVCVC-CV/ → cv(cvc$_{\mu}$)cv	*!		*
(ii) Moraic coda ☞	/CVC∅C-CV/ → cv(cvc$_{\mu}$)cv /CVCVC-CV/ → cv(cvc$_{\mu}$)cv		*	

Scenario (ii) is the winner as it satisfies moraic contiguity, even though it merges the V/∅ contrast on the surface.

Given the definition of MORA-CONTIGUITY, a non-moraic coda word-finally does not violate moraic contiguity, as it is edge-most in the string of segments.

(3-41) No violation of MORA-CONTIGUITY

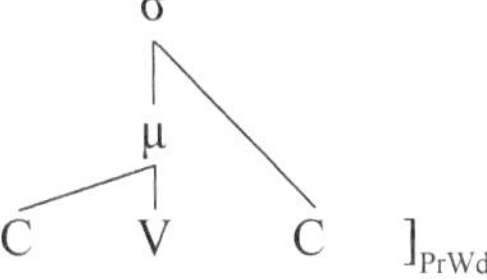

Thus, word-final epenthesis is contrast-preserving. This is illustrated in the following tableau.

(3-42) Final epenthesis – contrast is preserved

Scenarios		MORA CONTIGUITY	PC_{IN} (V/∅)	WBP	*FINAL FOOT
(i) Non-moraic coda ☞	/CVCVC-∅C/ → cv(cv́cvc) /CVCVC-VC/ → (cv́cv)cvc_{μ}			*	*
(ii) Moraic coda	/CVCVC-∅C/ → (cv́cv)cvc_{μ} /CVCVC-VC/ → (cv́cv)cvc_{μ}		*!		

Scenario (i) is the winner as it preserves contrast. Contiguity is not violated. The winning candidate also violates *FINALFOOT which is ranked below PC_{IN}(V/∅).

3.4.4 The typology

The core of the analysis is that the contrast in the presence vs. absence of a vowel is manifested as a surface contrast in prosodic prominence. This observation is accounted for in the framework of PC theory where contrast exists as an imperative in the grammar, formulated as a family of violable and rankable constraints on preserving contrasts. As has been shown, this analysis predicts the full typology of Arabic dialects, including contrast-preserving, contrast-neutralizing and hybrid dialects.

In contrast-preserving dialects (Syrian is the example used here), contrast is preserved at the expense of having a non-moraic coda. In terms of constraints, PC outranks WBP (see (3-43)). In contrast-neutralizing dialects (e.g. Omani), on the other hand, contrast preservation cannot compel a non-moraic coda. Thus, in Omani, WBP outranks PC (see (3-44)). Finally, in mixed dialects (e.g. Iraqi), contrast is preserved but only word-finally. MORA-CONTIGUITY outranks PC and thus medial non-moraic codas are ruled out, but PC outranks WBP so that the dialect is otherwise contrast-preserving (see 3-45).

(3-43) Contrast is preserved (Syrian) (section 3.4.1)
PC_{IN}(V/∅) >> WBP, MORA-CONTIGUITY

(3-44) Contrast is neutralized (Omani)[15] (section 3.4.2)
WBP >> PC_{IN}(V/∅)

(3-45) Contrast is preserved but only finally (Iraqi) (section 3.4.3)
MORA-CONTIGUITY >> PC_{IN}(V/∅) >> WBP

This provides a uniform account of contrast-preserving, contrast-neutralizing and mixed dialects. The core idea is that contrast preservation interacts with constraints on the moraic structure of syllables and moraic contiguity.

Contrast could also be preserved by simply not epenthesizing a vowel. To rule it out, I will assume that in all dialects you need epenthesis to avoid illicit clusters (Farwaneh 1995). In PC theory this means that a constraint forcing epenthesis,

*COMPLEX (no more than one C may associate to any syllable position node), dominates PC_{IN}(V/∅). This is illustrated below.[16]

(3-46) Epenthesis is enforced
*COMPLEX >> PC_{IN}(V/∅)

(3-47) Epenthesis takes place (see sections 3.4.1–3.4.3)

Scenarios		*COMPLEX	PC_{IN}(V/∅)
(i) Epenthesis ☞	/CVC∅C -CVC/ → CV.C**V**C.CVC /CVCVC-CVC/ → CV.CVC.CVC		*
(ii) No epenthesis	/CVC∅C -CVC/ → CVCC.CVC /CVCVC-CVC/ → CV.CVC.CVC	*!	

Scenario (i) with epenthesis is the winner. Scenario (ii) loses since it violates *COMPLEX.

In the next section, I discuss the prediction of the contrast analysis with respect to onset dialects.

3.5 Predictions for onset dialects

Dialects of Arabic are divided into onset and coda dialects. In onset dialects epenthesis creates an open syllable while in coda dialects the epenthetic syllable is closed. This section discusses the prediction of the proposal with respect to onset dialects.

It has been observed in Farwaneh (1995) that, unlike coda dialects, onset dialects are always contrast-neutralizing. That is, there is no difference in the way stress is assigned to epenthetic and non-epenthetic words. Egyptian Arabic (Broselow 1976, Farwaneh 1995, Harrell 1957) provides an example of an onset dialect. As shown below, in Egyptian Arabic, epenthetic and non-epenthetic words have the same stress. The epenthetic vowel is in bold font.

(3-48) Egyptian Stress
Epenthetic words

Example	**Gloss**	**Underlying**	**Reference**
a. bin(t**í**na)	'our daughter'	/bint-na/	F 135
b. ʔar(D**í**na)	'our land'	/ʔarD-na/	F 135
c. ʔis(m**í**ha)/ʔis(m**á**ha)	'her name'	/ʔism-ha/	H 84
d. dar(s**í**na)	'our lesson'	/dars-na/	H 84

Non-epenthetic words

Example	**Gloss**	**Underlying**	**Reference**
e. mad(rása)	'school'	/madrasa/	F 135
f. mar(tába)	'status'	/martaba/	F 135, H 15
g. kah(rába)	'electricity'	/kahraba/	H 73

Egyptian has a different stress pattern from dialects discussed so far. As described in Hayes (1995), it is a moraic trochee system with feet assigned from left to right. Main stress is located in the rightmost foot in the word. Some other examples of onset dialects are Sudanese (Hamid 1984, Trimingham 1946), and Saudi (Abu-Mansour 1987).

The key proposal developed in this book is that in contrast-preserving dialects the coda consonant of the syllable with an epenthetic vowel is non-moraic and therefore counts as light. This results in a different foot pattern of epenthetic and non-epenthetic words and thus different stress. Unlike previous approaches to stress-epenthesis interaction, this proposal predicts the non-contrast-preserving nature of epenthesis in onset dialects.

In onset dialects epenthesis creates an open syllable (Broselow 1982), as in /ʔarD-na/ → ʔar.Dí.na 'our land'. Since epenthesis creates an open syllable, there is no coda in the epenthetic syllable to deprive it of a mora and thus change stress. The epenthetic syllable only has an onset consonant which cannot have its own mora, and thus its moraicity will not affect stress placement. In effect, under the proposal developed here, onset dialects are not expected to assign stress differently to epenthetic and non-epenthetic words. The next section illustrates this prediction in more detail by taking into account locality of contrast preservation.

Before the proposal is developed further, let us discuss how OT generates onset and coda dialects. For earlier proposals, see Broselow (1982, 1992), Ito (1988, 1989), and Selkirk (1981), among others. A standard account of how coda/onset dialects are generated is a directionality account of Ito (1988, 1989). This account explains the site of epenthesis by selecting a directionality parameter for a given language: left to right in onset dialects and right to left in coda dialects (see Ito 1988: 191–199). An OT account of the onset/coda dialects is given in Mester and Padgett (1994) who propose to account for onset and coda dialects by different rankings of directional alignment constraints of the form SYLLABLE-ALIGN(Syllable, Edge, PrWd, Edge). The constraint is defined as "align every syllable edge x with some prosodic word edge x" (for more discussion of alignment, see McCarthy and Prince 1993, and McCarthy 2003c). In onset dialects, SYLLABLE-ALIGN(Syllable, L, PrWd, L) dominates SYLLABLE-ALIGN(Syllable, R, PrWd, R). In coda dialects, SYLLABLE-ALIGN(Syllable, L, PrWd, L) dominates SYLLABLE-ALIGN(Syllable, R, PrWd, R).

3.6 Locality of contrast preservation

In Arabic (and possibly universally in cases of contrast displacement), contrast is preserved locally. The moraless coda consonant occurs in the syllable with an epenthetic vowel and not in an adjacent syllable. Thus, contrast is being maintained *representationally* within the syllable. Following work on recoverability from the 1970s, local preservation of contrast increases recoverability since the output contrast remains closer to where contrast is expressed in the input.

To ensure locality of contrast preservation, Łubowicz (2003) develops a family of constraints on locality with respect to a prosodic domain, defined below. Such constraints restrict the domain where contrast is maintained representationally in the output.

(3-49) PC-DOMAIN(P)
Let In_1 and In_2 be minimally distinct in P
P-set = the set of all segments with properties P
In_1 = /…in-seg_i…/ ($seg_i \in$ P-set) and In_2 = /…in-seg_j…/ ($seg_j \notin$ P-set)
Let $In_1 \rightarrow Out_1$ and $In_2 \rightarrow Out_2$ (i.e. in-$seg_i \rightarrow$ out-seg_i)
If Out_1 and Out_2 are distinct representationally in some property Q
Q-set = the set of all segments with properties Q,
Out_1 = /…out-seg_k…/ ($seg_k \in$ Q-set) and Out_2 = /…out-seg_z…/ ($seg_z \notin$ Q-set)
then out-seg_k is contained in the same prosodic domain to which out-seg_i belongs (same for out-seg_z and out-seg_j).
Informally: "Do not move contrast out of its domain."

In Arabic the relevant prosodic domain is the syllable. The relevant constraint is PC-SYLLABLE(V/∅). The constraint PC-SYLLABLE(V/∅) in Arabic refers to structural contrast expression, which in this case is presence vs. absence of a mora. As we have seen, contrast in Arabic is ultimately realized in the output by the difference in stress via a different moraic structure of the coda of the epenthetic syllable. It is important to observe that the difference in moraicity is local though audible output contrast expression, stress, is realized on a different syllable than the epenthetic vowel.

The constraint on locality, PC-SYLLABLE(V/∅), needs to be ranked above the constraint on contrast preservation, PC_{IN}(V/∅), since in onset dialects contrast is neutralized to maintain locality.

(3-50) The ranking for locality[17]
PC-SYLLABLE(V/∅) >> PC_{IN}(V/∅)

The definition of PC-DOMAIN(P) requires that there is in-seg_i from which to calculate the domain for out-seg_i. Since we are talking about a V/∅ contrast, I will follow Wolf and McCarthy (2009) and assume that in comparing inputs and outputs we are looking at strings rather than individual segments. Thus, the empty spot is marked in the input indicated here with a null sign. It can be directly referred to in the formulation of constraints.[18]

The following tableau illustrates the ranking for locality of contrast preservation. It compares the actual contrast-neutralizing scenario and a competing contrast-preserving scenario in onset dialects. The contrast-preserving scenario preserves contrast but not in the same syllable as the epenthetic vowel. Consonantal moras are indicated in the output forms.

(3-51) The role of locality

Scenarios		PC-SYLLABLE(V/∅)	PC_{IN}(V/∅)	WBP
(i) Actual (contrast-neutralizing) ☞	dar_μ.(sí.na) mad_μ.(rá.sa)		*	
(ii) Contrast-preserving	(dár.**si**).na mad_μ.(rá.sa)	*!		*

The contrast-preserving scenario, scenario (ii), is ruled out by locality since it creates a moraless coda outside of the epenthetic syllable. It is more important to be local than to preserve contrast. Thus, onset dialects are predicted to be contrast neutralizing under this account.

This is a good prediction that is confirmed by the facts. I am not aware of any dialect in which the moraless coda is created outside of the epenthetic syllable. As will be discussed in the following section, previous approaches to stress-epenthesis interaction do not make this prediction.

3.7 Comparison with previous approaches

This section compares PC theory to other approaches to stress-epenthesis interaction proposed in the literature. Rule-based accounts are discussed in section 3.7.1, and other OT proposals in section 3.7.2.

3.7.1 Rule-based approaches

In contrast-preserving dialects, such as Syrian, the interaction of stress and epenthesis is opaque. That is, the way stress is assigned is inconsistent with the expected pattern. To recall, in word-medial epenthesis stress is antepenultimate (*ki.tá.**bit**.la*) and not penultimate (**ki.ta.**bít**.la*), as expected. Similarly, in word-final epenthesis, stress is penultimate (*ki.tá.**bit***) and not antepenultimate (**kí.ta.**bit***), as expected. In this section, I will discuss several rule-based approaches to stress-epenthesis interaction, including the rule-ordering approach (Kiparsky 1973), the representational approaches (Broselow 1992, Farwaneh 1995, Piggott 1995), and the invisibility approach (Michelson 1989).

A standard approach to opaque processes in rule-based theory is **rule ordering** (Kenstowicz and Kisseberth 1979, Kiparsky 1973, Rubach 1984). By rule ordering, in contrast-neutralizing dialects, epenthesis precedes stress assignment, and thus words with and without epenthesis have the same stress. In contrast-preserving dialects, on the other hand, stress precedes epenthesis, and thus words with and without epenthesis have different stress.

The rule-ordering approach is problematic for several reasons. To begin with, in this approach, it is difficult to explain cases like Iraqi Arabic, where epenthesis is contrast preserving but only word-finally. Word-medially contrast is merged. In the rule-ordering approach, we either preserve or neutralize contrast depending on the relative ordering of epenthesis and stress.

This problem has been already pointed out by Broselow (1982), who observes that one way to avoid it is to assume distinct epenthesis rules, one for word-final and the other for word-medial epenthesis, and to order them differently with respect to stress assignment. Specifically, word-medial epenthesis would precede stress assignment, and thus contrast would be merged word-medially. Word-final epenthesis, on the other hand, would follow stress assignment, and thus contrast would be preserved between epenthetic and non-epenthetic words in case of word-final epenthesis. But, as discussed in Broselow (1982), epenthesis into word-final and word-medial clusters has the same characteristics (Selkirk 1981), and so splitting of the epenthesis rule into two distinct processes is uncalled for. To solve this problem, rule-based accounts usually adopt an additional assumption of consonant extrametricality. With this assumption, epenthesis in word-final and word-medial positions will be one and the same process, but final consonants will be extrametrical at the point when stress applies. As a result, stress will precede word-final epenthesis. Post-lexically, extrametricality will be revoked and so final epenthesis will apply. But stress will have been assigned by then and thus epenthesis will be contrast-preserving word-finally. However, as shown in Prince and Smolensky (1993), formal extrametricality is problematic and should not be treated as a formal device. Prince and Smolensky argue that properties ascribed to formal extrametricality, such as nonexhaustivity, constituency, peripherality, edge markedness, and uniqueness, often encode some more general phonological tendencies and should be recognized as such (see Prince and Smolensky (1993: 44–47)).

Another generalization that is missed under the rule-based approach concerns onset dialects. It remains a mystery why all onset dialects are contrast-preserving in Arabic, unlike coda dialects, which are divided into contrast-preserving and contrast-neutralizing types. In rule ordering, this means that only one ordering of rules, epenthesis before stress assignment, is permitted for onset dialects. But why it should be so remains unexplained.

Broselow (1992) proposes a **representational account** of the same phenomena. She proposes that unsyllabified consonants are assigned the status of a monomoraic syllable in coda dialects (*ki.tab.*t_{μ}*.la*) and the status of an onset with an empty mora position in onset dialects (*ki.tab.t_.la*). In onset dialects the empty mora position is then filled with a vowel. This rightly predicts that words with and without epenthesis in onset dialects behave the same. In coda dialects, however, no vowel insertion is required. Therefore, words with and without epenthesis have different stress. For example, when epenthesis is into the penult, where the antepenultimate syllable is heavy, it is the antepenult that receives stress (*ki.táb.*t_{μ}*.la*). Subsequently, epenthesis and resyllabification take place and so stress assignment contradicts surface facts. This explains cases like Syrian, where stress in words with and without epenthesis is distinct.

Under this approach, contrast-neutralizing dialects like Omani seem problematic. That is, we need to explain why in some coda dialects epenthetic vowels count for stress. Another problem is to explain what forces epenthesis in this proposal. If the extrasyllabic consonant forms its own syllable, then there is no cluster within a syllable to be broken up by an epenthetic vowel.[19]

A difference in representation between epenthetic and non-epenthetic syllables has also been proposed in the literature by Piggott (1995), primarily on the basis of the analysis of Mohawk and some discussion of Iraqi Arabic. In Piggott's proposal, epenthetic syllables that behave exceptionally to stress assignment are represented as empty segmental slots, thus weightless, at the stage when stress rules apply. The empty slots are filled in at the later stages of derivation and thus surface with a vowel. This explains why open syllables can be exceptional to stress rules. Closed syllables, the ones that concern us here, are problematic under Piggott's proposal because, according to the so-called closed syllable condition formulated by Piggott, a closed syllable with a moraic coda cannot have an empty nucleus. Therefore, Piggott represents closed syllables with epenthetic vowels that do not count for stress as sequences of two syllables (for example the syllable ***bit*** as in *ki.ta.**bit**.la* is realized as ***bi**.t∅*). The surface coda consonant is realized as an onset consonant of the second syllable in the sequence (here *t∅*). This second syllable contains an empty nucleus at the stage when stress assignment takes place and is thus weightless. The syllable with an epenthetic vowel, the first syllable in the sequence (here ***bi***), is assigned a vowel with a mora under the so-called proper government condition, to avoid a sequence of two empty nuclei. Consequently, surface closed syllables count as light for purposes of stress rules.[20]

Despite the shared observation concerning the weight of closed epenthetic syllables in contrast-preserving languages, Piggott's account differs from my proposal in many respects. Piggott's proposal does not account for stress-epenthesis interaction in a surface approach to phonology, because it is not able to force epenthesis based on the well-formedness of the surface form alone. If we explain the light quality of the epenthetic syllable by allowing its coda consonant to form its own syllable, then there is no cluster within a syllable, and thus nothing forces epenthesis. The markedness constraint that drives epenthesis is satisfied with no repair. The surface form *ka.tab.t∅.la*, with no epenthesis, is optimal.

Farwaneh (1995) provides a solution in terms of **parameter choice**. In her proposal, unlike Broselow (1992), epenthetic syllables count as light in coda dialects until nucleus formation is invoked. Nucleus formation takes place iff the epenthetic syllable has an onset. She furthermore proposes that languages choose an option of either assigning an onset to the epenthetic syllables (*ka.ta.b_t.la*) or keeping the potential onset consonant in the coda of the preceding syllable (*ka.tab._t.la*). She captures this formally by allowing languages to choose either the so-called onset or weight-by-position parameter. Languages that choose the onset parameter merge the contrast between words with epenthetic and non-epenthetic vowels. Languages that choose the weight-by-position parameter retain the contrast. This can be seen in relation to resyllabification. That is, the onset parameter means that resyllabification takes place at the point when stress applies, whereas the weight-by-position parameter implies that resyllabification has not yet taken place. Since onsetless syllables do not have a nucleus when stress is assigned, this distinguishes between contrast-preserving and contrast-neutralizing dialects, a problem that Broselow's account faces.

This account does not seem to predict cases like Iraqi Arabic, where contrast is merged word-medially but preserved word-finally. Since contrast is merged for word-medial epenthesis, Iraqi would choose the onset parameter word-medially, thus surface *ki.ta.bít.la* would be syllabified *ki.ta.b_t.la* at the stage when stress applies (with the nucleus filled). By choosing the onset parameter, syllabification is the same as on the surface, and stress is assigned in the same way as to underlying vowels in the same position. But in word-final position, the onset parameter wrongly predicts antepenultimate stress, **kí.ta.b_t*, instead of the actual penultimate stress which is consistent with the WBP parameter, *ki.táb._t*. By choosing the WBP parameter, the penultimate syllable is heavy and thus receives stress. To account for cases of this type, we need to assume that a language can choose parameters depending on the site of epenthesis. In case of Iraqi, the onset parameter is chosen word-medially, but the WBP parameter word-finally. Unless there is some principled way of explaining this difference in the choice of the parameter, it should be avoided. Epenthesis is one process in Iraqi and should be formally captured as such.

Finally, let us discuss the **invisibility approach** to epenthesis developed by Michelson (1989), modifying Archangeli (1984). Using the example of Mohawk epenthesis, Michelson proposes that when words with epenthesis have different stress than words without epenthesis, epenthetic vowels are invisible to stress. The invisibility is achieved by proposing that in those cases epenthesis inserts segmental features without accompanying V-slots. V-slots give vowels the status of a nucleus. Thus, at the point when stress applies, epenthetic vowels do not have the status of a syllabic nucleus and so do not count for stress. In languages where epenthetic words behave the same as non-epenthetic words with respect to stress, on the other hand, V-slots are supplied before stress assignment takes place.

However, in languages where epenthesis improves syllable structure, as in Arabic, if V-slots are not present at the point when epenthesis takes place, then there is no reason for epenthesis. Vowels inserted without V-slots do not improve the syllable structure since they do not provide a nucleus and thus there seems to be no reason for inserting them. Therefore, this account finds it problematic to explain why epenthesis takes place in languages where it is syllable-driven.[21]

Just like the proposal in Farwaneh (1995), the invisibility hypothesis does not account for hybrid cases like Iraqi Arabic, unless we allow for separate V-slot rules depending on the environment of the epenthetic segment. Furthermore, under the invisibility proposal, onset dialects are left unexplained. That is, we expect onset dialects to either preserve or neutralize the underlying contrast on the surface depending on the ordering of V-slots insertion with respect to stress assignment. Yet, they are all contrast neutralizing. This would mean that in all onset dialects, V-slots assignment precedes stress. This seems accidental. Onset dialects present a problem for the rule-ordering accounts, as has been described in this section.

Unlike the approaches described above (the rule-ordering approach, the representational approaches, and the invisibility approach), PC theory gives a uniform account of contrast-preserving, contrast-neutralizing, and mixed dialects. It provides a solution to onset dialects being always contrast neutralizing and it also motivates epenthesis by avoiding consonant clusters.

3.7.2 OT approaches

In this section I discuss two OT approaches to stress-epenthesis interaction. One approach is by Alderete (1995, 1999) and involves special faithfulness constraints. The other approach is by Kiparsky (2000, 2002, to appear) and involves a derivational model of OT.

Alderete (1995, 1999) proposes that there exist faithfulness constraints that ban epenthetic vowels from bearing stress. These constraints are called HEAD-DEP and are defined below.

(3-52) HEAD-DEP (Alderete 1995)
Every segment contained in a prosodic head in S_2 (output) has a correspondent in S_1 (input).
"Epenthetic vowels cannot be stressed."

HEAD-DEP constraints have also been developed by Broselow (2001), Kager (1999a), and Revithiadou (1999).

Both PC theory and Alderete's account can result in epenthetic words having a different stress from non-epenthetic words. In Alderete's account this is achieved when a faithfulness constraint HEAD-DEP dominates constraints on stress assignment. In Arabic, along the lines developed in this chapter, epenthetic words have different stress when HEAD-DEP outranks WBP. This is illustrated in the following tableau. The tableau evaluates stress of an epenthetic form /kitab-t-la/ in which epenthesis creates a closed penultimate syllable. A contrast-preserving form *ki(tábit)la* with irregular stress is compared to a contrast-neutralizing form *kita(bít$_\mu$)la* with regular stress.

(3-53) The role of HEAD-DEP

	/kitab-t-la/	HEAD-DEP	WBP
a. Contrast preserving ☞	ki(tábit)la		*
b. Contrast neutralizing	kita(bít$_\mu$)la	*!	

For the contrast-preserving form to be optimal, HEAD-DEP must outrank WBP, forcing a violation of it. With the opposite ranking, WBP over HEAD-DEP, epenthesis would be contrast neutralizing (provided that no other higher-ranked constraint forces a violation of WBP).

There is a crucial difference between Alderete's account and PC theory. Unlike the contrast account, Alderete's approach cannot explain cases where epenthesis is contrast preserving for reasons other than avoiding the HEAD-DEP violation. These are cases where stress in words with and without epenthesis is distinct, but the epenthetic vowel would not be stressed, even if epenthetic words received regular stress. Word-final epenthesis in Iraqi Arabic provides an example. Neither the contrast-preserving form *ki(tábit)* with irregular stress nor the contrast-neutralizing form *(kíta)bit* with regular stress violate HEAD-DEP. Since the epenthetic vowel is not stressed in either case, there is no violation of HEAD-DEP, and thus something else must compel the irregular stress of epenthetic words. In the contrast account, this is due to the constraint on preserving contrasts between epenthetic and non-epenthetic words.[22]

Moreover, PC and Alderete's approaches make different predictions with respect to the ways in which the contrast between epenthetic and non-epenthetic words can be manifested. Alderete's account predicts that if the epenthetic and non-epenthetic words are different, the difference is in stress while PC theory predicts that other differences are possible. The predictions of PC theory are more accurate. There are cases reported in the literature where the differences between epenthetic and non-epenthetic words take the form other than stress. For example, Broselow (2001) argues that hollow verbs in Iraqi Arabic change the quality of the epenthetic vowel in order to express contrast. See the references in section 3.1.

Kiparsky (2000, 2002, to appear) develops a different proposal for stress-epenthesis interaction based on the lexical phonology model of OT (LPM-OT). Like Broselow (1992), Kiparsky posits a special structure for epenthetic syllables at the lexical (word) level in contrast-preserving dialects. It is proposed that in those dialects stray consonants are licensed as semi-syllables at the word level, directly adjoined to a PrWd node rather than a syllable node. Consequently, there is no need for epenthesis at that level since there are no consonant clusters. This structure is then readjusted post-lexically by epenthesis. But stress has already applied at the word level. As a result, epenthetic vowels are opaque to stress. To take an example, underlying */fihm-na/* 'our understanding' maps onto word-level *(fíh)m-na* with no epenthesis. Stress applies at this level but does not see epenthetic syllables since they are not there. Subsequently, the same structure maps onto post-lexical *fíhim-na* with epenthetic *i* and stress is carried over from the word stratum. Thus, in those dialects epenthetic vowels are opaque to stress. This is achieved by positing distinct constraint rankings for word and post-lexical levels of representation by which in contrast-preserving dialects semi-syllables exist at the lexical level, as ***m*** in *(fíh)**m**-na*, and are repaired at the post-lexical level by epenthesis, as in *fíh**i**m-na*. In contrast-neutralizing dialects, on the other hand, semi-syllables are not allowed and so epenthetic vowels count for stress. Thus, in this account of Arabic, opacity follows from the ordering of levels and special assumptions about epenthetic syllables.

Similar to representational approaches described in section 3.7.1, this approach does not predict why onset dialects will always be contrast neutralizing. To account for the same stress of epenthetic and non-epenthetic words in onset dialects, this model proposes that in all onset dialects semi-syllables are ruled out at all levels and thus epenthesis needs to take place before stress assignment. Consequently, epenthetic words have the same stress as non-epenthetic words. Moreover, without additional assumptions, this approach does not predict hybrid cases as in Iraqi

Arabic. In this chapter, I have developed a very different approach from Kiparsky's to stress-epenthesis interaction, based on a parallel model of OT, and investigated its implications.

3.8 Conclusion

This chapter has provided a contrast analysis of stress-epenthesis interaction in Arabic dialects. The key idea is that in contrast-preserving dialects, the underlying contrast in the presence vs. absence of a vowel is manifested as a surface stress contrast. This observation has been captured formally in the framework of PC theory (Łubowicz 2003).

In PC theory contrast preservation exists as an imperative in the grammar which is expressed as a family of rankable and violable constraints on preserving contrasts, called PC constraints. In contrast-preserving dialects, a PC constraint against neutralization of the contrast between epenthetic and non-epenthetic words compels the non-moraic coda consonant in the epenthetic syllable. This leads to a different foot structure of a word and consequently different stress (section 3.4).

The contrast analysis is argued to be superior to previous approaches. First, it provides a uniform account of stress-epenthesis interaction in Arabic dialects, including hybrid cases as in Iraqi Arabic (section 3.4.3). Second, it predicts the non-contrast-preserving nature of onset epenthesis (sections 3.5 and 3.6). Last but not least, unlike previous approaches, PC theory allows distinctions between epenthetic and non-epenthetic words to be expressed in more ways than simply by a difference in stress (section 3.7.2).

Notes

1. For orthographic convenience, emphatic consonants are transcribed as upper case Cs.
2. An alternative would be to propose that the epenthetic syllable is light because the epenthetic vowel is moraless. This alternative would not work here because there would be no reason to epenthesize a moraless vowel. Epenthesis in Arabic is motivated by improving syllable structure and a moraless vowel does not improve syllable structure. See section 3.7 for more in depth discussion of this alternative and why it doesn't work.
3. This is under the assumption that correspondence is also established for segment/zero contrasts (Wolf and McCarthy 2009).
4. In PC theory (Łubowicz 2003) scenarios are sets of forms but for the understanding of the argument presented in this chapter, pairs of forms are sufficient.
5. In most (if not all) cases a difference in a representational property (an unhearable contrast) would translate into a difference in an audible or phonetic property. Also, if a language does not normally assign moras to coda consonants, it can still use stress shift to maintain contrast. As long as epenthetic and non-epenthetic outputs are distinct in stress or some other audible property in this language, the $PC_{IN}(V/\emptyset)$ constraint is satisfied. Thanks to the anonymous reviewer for questions on this point.
6. I assume that a heavy syllable coda is linked to a different mora than the preceding vowel (see representation in (3-36)).

7. There is a competing scenario that places stress on the epenthetic vowel. In this scenario stress is on the final syllable in the epenthetic form and on the ante-penultimate syllable in the non-epenthetic form: /CVCVC-∅C/ → cvcv(cv̍c_{μ}), /CVCVC-VC/ → (cv̍cv)cvc_{μ}. This candidate satisfies PC because epenthetic and non-epenthetic forms have different stress. It also satisfies WBP because the final syllable is heavy. This candidate violates a constraint that bans prominence from appearing on the final syllable, NonFinal(Prom). To rule it out, it must be more important to avoid placing stress on the final syllable than to create non-moraic codas: NonFinal(Prom) >> WBP.
8. Northern Omani has a different stress pattern (see Qafisheh 1977).
9. I have also consulted a native speaker of northern Omani. Northern Omani has a different stress pattern. In the case of two final light syllables, stress falls on the penultimate syllable and not on the antepenultimate syllable. Interestingly, the generalization holds of both epenthetic and non-epenthetic words. Compare epenthetic sa.raq.lá.ħin 'he stole a tune' with non-epenthetic sa.raq.sá.ħib 'he stole a friend'.
10. The epenthetic vowel is realized as [i] or [u] depending on the environment. The rounded vowel occurs in the neighborhood of labials, emphatics, velars, and r.
11. For other cases of mixed weight systems, see Rosenthall and van der Hulst (1999).
12. Variable closed syllable weight is also discussed in Rosenthall and van der Hulst (1999). They describe cases where closed syllables are light but contextually heavy and cases where closed syllables are heavy but contextually light. Similar to the analysis in this chapter, in their proposal contextually dependent weight is a result of the interaction of violable and rankable constraints.
13. As will be shown, Mora-Contiguity will play an essential role in establishing the typology of stress-epenthesis interaction.
14. Under a different assumption, where the coda consonant is adjoined to the mora of the preceding vowel, mora-contiguity would need to be reformulated so that it is violated even when the coda consonant shares a mora with a preceding vowel.

    Definition of Mora-Contiguity (possible revision)
    In αβδ where β is in coda position, if $\alpha \in \mu$ and $\delta \in \mu$, then $\beta \in \mu$ and this mora belongs exclusively to β.

15. Here, the ranking of Mora-Contiguity is not crucial.
16. In addition, to ensure that we do not satisfy *Complex by deleting a consonant, we need a PC_{IN}(C/∅) constraint that outranks PC_{IN}(V/∅). The ranking of PC_{IN}(C/∅) over PC_{IN}(V/∅) is a central property of Arabic: vowels come and go, but consonants abide.
17. To prevent generating dialects in which the moraless coda is outside of the epenthetic syllable, the ranking between locality and PC needs to be fixed (also known as meta-ranking or fixed ranking). There are several ways to think about locality in Arabic. One possibility which is outlined here is by having a separate locality constraint universally ranked about PC (fixed ranking). But this requirement could also be part of constraints on contrast themselves. Another possibility would be to assume that the alternative candidate in Arabic would violate alignment constraints on stress assignment (Align-R) which would then outrank PC. I do not choose the latter alternative because this alternative would allow some languages to preserve contrast non-locally under a different ranking of PC and Align-R and I don't know of any cases like that. All cases discussed in this book, including Arabic, chain shifts, and allomorphy, preserve contrast locally.
18. The proposal developed by Wolf and McCarthy (2009) is called string-based correspondence.

19. Despite the problems in predictions noted above, Broselow (1992) provides an explanation of how onset and coda dialects are generated.
20. An extension and refinement of the analysis of weightless epenthetic vowels in Piggott (1995) is provided in Piggott (1998).
21. This is under the assumption that *COMPLEX is violated by a sequence of consonants separated by a moraless vowel. For vowels that are not true segments, see Browman and Goldstein (1986), Gafos (2002), and Hall (2003).
22. Broselow (2001) breaks the HEAD-DEP constraint into two sets of constraints. She distinguishes between HEADSYLL-DEP (epenthetic vowels cannot be stressed) and HEADFOOT-DEP (epenthetic vowels cannot be anywhere in a main-stressed foot). This does not change the fact that contrast-preserving epenthesis in word-final position as in Iraqi and Omani is problematic. In fact, the constraint that prohibits epenthetic vowels from the main-stressed foot rules out the actual form *ki(tábit)* because it bans a foot that contains an epenthetic vowel. This point is also made by Broselow (2001).

4 Morphological contrast

This chapter extends the proposal to morphological contrast by investigating the role of contrast in the surface distribution of allomorphs. The case study is allomorph distribution in the locative of masculine and neuter nouns in Polish. It is shown that locative allomorph distribution is opaque and can be accounted for in terms of preserving contrast. The key idea is that the different allomorphs of the locative suffix keep apart forms that the regular phonology would otherwise neutralize. This contributes to our understanding of opaque allomorphy and the role of contrast.

4.1 Introduction

The study of allomorphy has received considerable attention in Optimality Theory (hereafter OT) (Prince and Smolensky 1993/2004). There is a research program in OT which accounts for allomorphy in terms of the well-formedness of the output. Allomorph distribution has been shown to be determined by phonological factors, such as *stress* (Anttila 1997, Drachman *et al.* 1995, Kager 1996, Mester 1994), *syllable structure* (Bonet 2004, Hargus and Tuttle 1997, Łubowicz *et al.* 2007, Mascaró 1996, McCarthy and Prince 1993, Prince and Smolensky 1993/2004, Rubach and Booij 2001, Tranel 1996, 1998), and *phonotactics* (Anttila 2002, Bermúdez-Otero 2007, Oostendorp 1998, Yip 2004).[1]

Allomorphy that cannot be explained by the properties of the output (Kiparsky 1997, Oostendorp 1998), which I will call *opaque allomorphy*, seemingly presents a problem for this line of research. This chapter proposes a solution to opaque allomorphy in this research program in terms of preserving contrast. For related approaches, see Gafos and Ralli (2002), Kenstowicz (2005), Kurisu (1998), McCarthy (2005), Rebrus and Törkenczy (2005), Steriade (1997, 2000), and Urbanczyk (1998, 1999).

This chapter investigates the role of contrast in allomorph selection. The case study is locative allomorphy of masculine and neuter nouns in Polish (Feldstein and Franks 2002, Grzegorczykowa *et al.* 1984, Gussmann 1980, Jaworski 1986, Rubach 1984, Szober 1969, among others). It is argued that the distribution of the locative allomorphs is opaque and can be determined by paradigmatic contrast. The key idea is that the different allomorphs of the locative suffix preserve contrasts that would be otherwise neutralized on the surface due to palatalization. The analysis is couched within the framework of PC theory introduced in the previous chapters, which is extended to the area of allomorphy. This study contributes to our understanding of morphological opacity and the role for contrast.[2]

The rest of this chapter is organized as follows. Section 4.2 describes the problem. Section 4.3 outlines the proposal. Section 4.4 presents the solution. Section 4.5 discusses typological predictions of the proposal and compares it with alternatives. Finally, section 4.6 is the conclusion.

4.2 Statement of the problem

In Polish, there is a process of coronal palatalization (Gussmann 1980, Rubach 1984), by which alveolars and dentals turn into prepalatals before front vowels (see section 4.4). The following are examples of palatalization before the locative singular suffix [-e]. Below, I illustrate the alternations with the nominative singular and locative singular of masculine and neuter nouns in Polish. For the purposes of the presentation of the argument, I do not indicate final devoicing. I will be consistent with this throughout the chapter.[3]

(4-1) Coronal palatalization: /t d n s z/ → [ć dź ń ś ź]/_e

		nominative sg.	**locative sg.**	**gloss**
t → ć	:	lis[t]	o liś[ć] + e	'letter'
d → dź	:	obia[d]	o obie[dź] + e	'dinner'
n → ń	:	ok[n] + o	o ok[ń] + e	'window'
s → ś	:	bruda[s]	o bruda[ś] + e	'dirty man'
z → ź	:	łobu[z]	o łobu[ź] + e	'troublemaker'

Interestingly, underlying prepalatals take the back high vowel [-u] suffix in the locative and not the front mid vowel [-e] suffix. Again, I show the examples in the nominative singular and the locative singular of masculine and neuter nouns.

(4-2) Original prepalatals

		nominative sg.	**locative sg.**	**gloss**
ć	:	liś[ć]	o liś[ć] + u	'leaf'
dź	:	narzę[dź] + e	o narzę[dź] + u	'tool'
ń	:	ko[ń]	o ko[ń] + u	'horse'
ś	:	łoso[ś]	o łoso[ś] + u	'salmon'
ź	:	pa[ź]	o pa[ź] + u	'type of butterfly'

This is an example of opaque allomorphy. As shown in (4-1) and (4-2), there are two allomorphs for the locative singular suffix, [-e] and [-u]. The selected allomorph cannot be determined from the surface form alone, The core observation is that the choice of the locative allomorph depends on whether the prepalatal in stem final position is underlying or derived. Derived prepalatals, as in (4-1), take the [-e] ending, while original prepalatals, as in (4-2), take the [-u] ending.[4]

The main question this raises is why original and derived prepalatals take different suffixes in the locative. In an output-oriented approach to phonology, such as OT, there should be no difference between underlying and derived prepalatals in their choice of the allomorph. Since derived and underlying prepalatals are articulated in the output in the same way (Wierzchowska 1971), they should select the same suffix in the locative. I will provide an explanation for why original and derived prepalatals take different suffixes in the locative using the principle of contrast.

The key argument is that the allomorph distribution in the locative, [-e] vs. [-u], preserves the original contrast between dentals/alveolars vs. prepalatals in stem final position: /list/ vs. /liść/ map onto [liść + e] vs. [liść + u]. If both forms took the same suffix [-e], the contrast between them would be neutralized on the surface due to palatalization: /list/ vs. /liść/ would both map onto [liść + e]. To put it differently, the original contrast between alveolars/dentals vs. prepalatals is preserved on the surface and manifested as a surface contrast in the choice of the allomorph, [-e] vs. [-u], respectively. The original contrast in the quality of the stem-final consonant is transformed into a surface contrast in the choice of the locative suffix.

There are numerous forms in Polish morphophonology where the contrast between inputs that differ in palatalization is preserved in the output and realized by the choice of a different suffix allomorph. Similar to the locative of masculine and neuter nouns shown in (4-1)–(4-2), in the dative and locative of feminine nouns, underlying dental/alveolar and prepalatal consonants take different allomorphs in the output: /kas + a/ vs. /kaś + a/ map onto [kaś + e] vs. [kaś + i], respectively. In effect, contrast is preserved between input forms that differ in the quality of the stem-final consonant despite palatalization.

(4-3) [-e] vs. [-i/ɨ] allomorphy (dative and locative of feminine nouns)

a. Coronal palatalization

		nominative sg.	**dative sg.**	**gloss**
t → ć	:	pso[t] + a	pso[ć] + e	'prank'
d → dź	:	wo[d] + a	wo[dź] + e	'water'
n → ń	:	stro[n] + a	stro[ń] + e	'page'
s → ś	:	ka[s] + a	ka[ś] + e	'register'
z → ź	:	ska[z] + a	ska[ź] + e	'shortcoming'

b. Original prepalatals

		nominative sg.	**dative sg.**	**gloss**
ć	:	kość[ć]	koś[ć] + i	'bone'
dź	:	łó[dź]	ło[dź] + i	'boat'
ń	:	baś[ń]	baś[ń] + i	'fairy tale'
ś	:	ka[ś]+a	ka[ś] + i	'proper name'
ź	:	ma[ź]	ma[ź] + i	'sticky substance'

The different allomorphs for underlying dentals/alveolars and prepalatals are also present in the nominative plural of masculine nouns (see (4-4)) and in the nominative singular of neuter nouns (see (4-5)).

(4-4) [-e] vs. [-ɨ] allomorphy (nom. pl. of masculine non-personal inanimate nouns)

a. Non-palatals

		nominative sg.	**nominative pl.**	**gloss**
t	:	bile[t]	bile[t] + ɨ	'tickets'
d	:	ko[d]	ko[d] + ɨ	'code'
n	:	dzwo[n]	dzwo[n] + ɨ	'bell'
s	:	intere[s]	intere[s] + ɨ	'business'
z	:	wó[z]	wo[z] + ɨ	'cart, waggon'

b. Original prepalatals

		nominative sg.	**nominative pl.**	**gloss**
ć	:	liś[ć]	liś[ć] + e	'leaf'
dź	:	gwóź[dź]	gwoź[dź] + e	'nail'
ń	:	kamie[ń]	kamie[ń] + e	'stone'
ś	:	łoso[ś]	łoso[ś] + e	'salmon'
ź	:	pa[ź]	pa[ź] + e	'type of butterfly'

(4-5) [-o] vs. [-e] allomorphy (nom. sg. of neuter nouns)

a. Non-palatals

		nominative sg.	**gloss**	
t	:	la[t] + o	'summer'	
d	:	gniaz[d] + o	'nest'	
n	:	ziar[n] + o	'seed'	
s	:	mię[s] + o	'meat'	
z	:	awi[z] + o	'notification, notice'	(or awiz)

b. Original prepalatals

		nominative sg.	**gloss**
ć	:	przejś[ć] + e	'passage'
dź	:	narzę[dź] + e	'tool'
ń	:	nasie[ń] + e	'seed'
ś	:	pro[ś] + ę	'young pig'
ź	:	podwo[ź] + e	'under-carriage'

Though the details of the distribution in the above paradigms differ from the leading example, they further support the observation that the height contrast is preserved in Polish morphophonology. In all cases, original prepalatals take different allomorphs than underlying dental/alveolar consonants.

An output-oriented approach to phonology, such as OT, offers new insights into the Polish declension pattern. In the next section I will apply PC theory, introduced in Chapters 2 and 3, to Polish allomorphy.

4.3 PC theory review

As has been shown in previous chapters, contrast plays an essential role in a number of phonological and morphological processes. This chapter investigates the role of contrast in allomorph selection. In the Polish locative, the key claim is that the grammar maintains contrast between forms that the regular phonology would otherwise neutralize. Specifically, forms that are distinct in the stem-final consonant in the input take different suffixes in the locative, and thus map onto distinct outputs. The analysis will be couched within the framework of PC theory laid out in Chapter 2. In the rest of this section I describe the elements of PC theory that are relevant for allomorphy. I first describe the candidate over which contrast is evaluated and then discuss the constraints that evaluate contrast.

4.3.1 The candidate

To evaluate contrast, a candidate is a set of input–output mappings, called a scenario (see references in previous chapters). Below is the actual scenario in Polish over which contrast is evaluated. Forms that contrast in the quality of the stem final consonant, li[st] vs. li[ść], take different suffixes in the locative, [-e] vs. [-u], respectively. The contrasts are represented in bold font.

(4-6) The actual scenario (cf. (4-1) and (4-2))

Input		**Output**
li**st**, {+e, +u}	⟶	liść + **e**
li**ść**, {+e, +u}	⟶	liść + **u**

In case of affix allomorphy, the inputs of the scenario consist of a set of stems and allomorphs. The allomorphs are language-particular. In Polish, it is a set of two vowels {+e, +u}. Thus, each stem has a choice between [-e] or [-u] in the locative. It is standard to assume that the idiosyncratic allomorphs are listed in the lexicon. Since the choice of either [-e] or [-u] is unpredictable from the surface form of the stem, allomorphs must be stored in the lexicon as a set.

The input also contains stems to which allomorphs attach. Following discussion in Chapter 2, I propose that input strings to which allomorphs attach are generated by the function Gen, similar to Gen in Correspondence Theory (McCarthy and Prince 1995). Gen takes an input string and emits a set of forms. The forms generated by Gen consist of any combination of phonological properties P which are essentially any properties governed by standard faithfulness constraints (Prince and Smolensky 1993/2004), such as height, place of articulation, voicing, and so on. Each form from the set of input strings generated by Gen is paired up with the language-particular set of allomorphs. These are the inputs of a scenario, as represented below.

(4-7) The inputs of a scenario
Gen(list, {+e, +u}) = list, {+e, +u}; liść, {+e, +u}; teść, {+e, +u} etc.

The output of a scenario is a subset of the input. There is nothing in the output that is not also in the input. Gen pairs up each input with an output form.

In effect, scenarios represent various mapping coexistence patterns. The scenario is a candidate, and thus, the actual scenario is compared to other scenarios in the same candidate set. Below are two competing scenarios in the Polish locative, the actual scenario and a contrast-neutralizing scenario.

(4-8) Scenarios in a candidate set

Scenario	Actual		Contrast-neutralizing	
Output	[liść + e]	[liść + u]	[liść + e]	
	↑	↑	↑	↖
Input	/list, {+e, +u}/	/liść , {+e, +u}/	/list, {+e, +u}/	/liść, {+e, +u}/

The scenarios above differ on the set of outputs. In the actual scenario, contrast is preserved between stems ending in dentals/alveolars vs. prepalatals: /list/ vs. /liść/ map onto [liść + e] vs. [liść + u]. In the contrast-neutralizing scenario, stems ending in dentals/alveolars vs. prepalatals are not distinguishable: /list/ vs. /liść / both map onto [liść + e]. (There are other scenarios that need to be considered; see section 4.5.)

As explained in Chapter 2, scenarios are submitted for evaluation to Eval. The optimal scenario is chosen by the constraints on contrast interacting with each other and with conflicting markedness constraints. There are also constraints on recoverability (see Chapter 3). In this model, following previous work on allomorphy in OT, allomorph distribution is controlled by universal and violable constraints but allomorphs themselves need to be stored in the lexicon. A major contribution of this work is that the principle of contrast plays a crucial role in allomorph selection.

4.3.2 Constraints on contrast

In generative phonology, contrast is a derivative of the grammar but there is increasing evidence that contrast exists as a separate principle in the grammar (see references in Chapter 1).

The core claim of this proposal is that contrast exists as an imperative in the phonological system. In OT, this is formulated as a family of rankable and violable constraints on preserving contrasts, called PC constraints. The definitions are recalled below (see Chapter 2 for discussion).

(4-9) $PC_{IN}(P)$
For each pair of inputs contrasting in P that map onto the same output in a scenario, assign a violation mark. Formally, assign one mark for every pair of inputs, in_a and in_b, if in_a has P and in_b lacks P, $in_a \rightarrow out_k$, and $in_b \rightarrow out_k$.

"If inputs are distinct in P, they need to remain distinct in the output (not necessarily in P)."

The definition of what it means to contrast in P is given below.

(4-10) Contrast in P
A pair of forms, in_a and in_b, contrast in P when corresponding segments in those forms, seg_a and seg_b, are such that seg_a has P and seg_b lacks P (same for outputs).

PC_{IN} constraints require that forms that contrast in phonological property P in the input contrast on the surface in some way.

One of the most crucial properties of PC constraints is that unlike standard faithfulness, PC constraints allow a given underlying contrast to be realized as a different surface contrast. In the Polish locative, the underlying contrast in the quality of the stem-final consonant is manifested as a surface contrast in the quality of the allomorph (see (4-6)).

Finally, as will be shown below, PC constraints together with other constraints can determine which allomorph is selected in the output and in that respect resemble markedness constraints. As discussed in Kager (1999b), faithfulness constraints cannot determine allomorph selection under the assumption that both allomorphs are present in the input.

As was explained in previous chapters, there are no standard faithfulness constraints in PC theory. A lot of work of faithfulness is subsumed under contrast. But in addition to constraints on contrast, there are recoverability constraints and generalized faithfulness in stage 2 of Eval, which resolve ties among candidates. It is an important observation that contrast and markedness are not enough to make effective comparisons between candidates.

4.4 The analysis

This section presents the analysis. I first present the core argument (4.4.1), followed by allomorph distribution (4.4.2), the role of contrast (4.4.3), and a summary of the analysis (4.4.4).

4.4.1 Core argument

As shown in section 4.2, the front vowel allomorph [-e] causes palatalization of the preceding consonant. This is referred to as coronal palatalization (Rubach 1984). According to coronal palatalization, anterior consonants such as dentals and alveolars /s z t d n/ turn into prepalatals [ś ź ć dź ń] before front vocoids [i], [e], and [j]. This is stated as follows:

(4-11) Coronal palatalization
[+anterior, +coronal] → prepalatal / ________ [-cons, –back][5]

Examples are repeated below.

(4-12) Coronal Palatalization (cf. (4-1))

		nominative sg.	**locative sg.**	**gloss**
t → ć	:	lis[t]	o liś[ć] + e	'letter'
d → dź	:	obia[d]	o obie[dź] + e	'dinner'
n → ń	:	ok[n] + o	o ok[ń] + e	'window'
s → ś	:	bruda[s]	o bruda[ś] + e	'dirty man'
z → ź	:	łobu[z]	o łobu[ź] + e	'troublemaker'

Palatalization is an example of assimilation, where the consonant takes on some of the articulatory properties of the following vowel (see Ćavar 2004, Gussmann 1980, Kochetov 2001, Rubach 1981, 1984, 2003).

Rubach (1984) describes prepalatals as [+high, –back]. Phonetically speaking, prepalatals are "(…) produced with the body of the tongue in the front position. The tongue is tense and the lips are spread. The air escapes through a very narrow channel made between the post-alveolar region of the palate and the middle of the tongue" (Puppel *et al.* 1977, cited in Ladefoged and Maddieson 1996: 155; see also Keating 1988, Styczek 1973, and Wierzchowska 1971).

To account for palatalization, I propose that there exists a markedness constraint against the sequence of an anterior coronal followed by a front vowel (*se, *ze, *te, etc.), called PAL. As a result of palatalization, the contrast is neutralized between underlying and derived prepalatals. I will refer to this contrast as a contrast in height. This is because prepalatals and the sounds prepalatals come from (dentals and alveolars) are differently specified for [αhigh].[6]

For palatalization to take place, the markedness constraint PAL must outrank the constraint on preserving contrast between underlying and derived prepalatals, called PC_{IN}(high). The constraints and their ranking are given below.

(4-13) PAL
No anterior coronal followed by a front vowel.

(4-14) PC_{IN}(high)
For each pair of inputs contrasting in height that map onto the same output in a scenario, assign a violation mark.
"If inputs are distinct in height, they need to remain distinct in the output."

(4-15) Palatalization ranking
PAL >> PC_{IN}(high)

In effect, palatalization neutralizes the height contrast. This is represented in the following tableau. I compare two scenarios, one without palatalization, the contrast-preserving scenario (i), and one with palatalization, the contrast-neutralizing scenario (ii). The forms are hypothetical and are meant to illustrate the consequences of palatalization in a phonological system.

(4-16) Palatalization neutralizes the height contrast

	Scenarios	PAL	PC_{IN}(high)
(i) Contrast-preserving	/pas + e/ → pas + e /paś + e/ → paś + e	*!	
(ii) Contrast-neutralizing ☞	/pas + e/ → paś + e /paś + e/ → paś + e		*

The scenario which fails to palatalize, scenario (i), is eliminated. It incurs a fatal violation of PAL. The contrast-neutralizing scenario wins since it undergoes palatalization. With the opposite ranking, PC_{IN}(high) >> PAL, no palatalization would take place.

The key observation in this chapter, as described in section 4.2, is that locative allomorphy preserves the height contrast between derived and original prepalatals. This height contrast is preserved on the surface despite palatalization and realized by different suffixes. As illustrated in (4-1) and (4-2), underlying prepalatals take the [-e] allomorph while derived prepalatals take the [-u] allomorph. Thus, allomorphy preserves the contrast between underlying and derived prepalatals despite palatalization. This is represented schematically below.

(4-17) The role for allomorphy (cf. (4-6))

Input		**Output**
lis**t**, {+e, +u}	——→	liść + **e**
liś**ć**, {+e, +u}	——→	liść + **u**

The choice of the allomorph keeps apart forms that would be neutralized on the surface due to palatalization. To put it differently, the original contrast in height, [lis**t**] vs. [liś**ć**], is manifested as a surface contrast in the choice of the allomorph, [-e] vs. [-u].

Below I compare three scenarios: scenario (i), in which both forms have the same allomorph [-e]; scenario (ii), in which the two forms have different allomorphs, [-e] and [-u]; and scenario (iii) which fails to palatalize.[7]

(4-18) Allomorphy preserves the contrast in height

	Scenarios	PAL	PC_{IN}(high)
(i) Contrast-neutralizing	/list, {+e, +u}/ → liść + e /liść, {+e, +u}/ → liść + e		*!
(ii) Contrast-preserving ☞ (=Actual)	/list, {+e, +u}/ → liść + e /liść, {+e, +u}/ → liść + u		
(iii) Contrast-preserving	/list, {+e, +u}/ → list + e /liść, {+e, +u}/ → liść + e	*!	

Scenario (i) is eliminated since it neutralizes the contrast in height. In this scenario, two distinct underlying forms map onto the same output, and thus are not distinguished from one another. Scenario (iii) fails since it does not palatalize and thus incurs a fatal violation of PAL. Scenario (ii) is chosen as optimal since it palatalizes but also keeps apart the two distinct underlying forms. In terms of constraints, scenario (ii) satisfies both PAL and PC_{IN}(high).

The constraint PC_{IN}(high) is satisfied in scenario (ii) because the two inputs, [list] vs. [liść], that contrast in the height of the stem-final consonant, [t] vs. [ć], contrast in the output in the quality of the suffix vowel, [-e] vs. [-u]. As will be discussed in section 4.4.3, PC constraints allow for contrast transformation where a given input contrast is manifested in the output in a different way than in the input.

In summary, though palatalization can neutralize the height contrast (see tableau (4-16)), the locative allomorphy preserves the height contrast, despite palatalization (see tableau (4-18)). In effect, allomorphy keeps apart forms that the regular phonology would otherwise neutralize. In Polish, allomorphy compensates for palatalization.

In addition to derived prepalatals, there exist underlying prepalatals in Polish. Consider the following minimal pairs:

(4-19) a. Underlying dental/alveolar

te[st]	'test'
li[st]	'letter'
ka[s] + a	'register'

b. Underlying prepalatal

te[ść]	'father in law'
li[ść]	'leaf'
Ka[ś] + a	'Kate'

Since there are underlying prepalatals in Polish, it must be the case that the constraint on preserving the contrast in height dominates the constraint against prepalatals, which I will call *[+high, –back]. This is represented below.

(4-20) *[+high, –back]
No prepalatals.

(4-21) Prepalatals surface
PC_{IN}(high) >> *[+high, –back]

According to the ranking above, underlying prepalatals are present in the output forms in Polish. This is represented in the following tableau. I compare two scenarios, a contrast-preserving scenario, scenario (i), in which the underlying contrast in height is preserved in the output, and a contrast-neutralizing scenario, scenario (ii), where there are no prepalatals in the output.

(4-22) Underlying prepalatals exist[8]

	Scenarios	PC_{IN}(high)	*[+high, –back]
(i) Contrast-preserving ☞	/test/ → test /teść / → teść		*
(ii) Contrast-neutralizing	/test/ → test /teść / → test	*!	

Scenario (i), in which prepalatals surface, is the winner. It satisfies PC_{IN}(high) at the expense of segmental markedness. Scenario (ii) is eliminated, since it neutralizes the contrast in height.

Altogether, the ranking is as follows:

(4-23) PAL >> PC_{IN}(high) >> *[+high, –back]

Underlying prepalatals exist but palatalization can neutralize the contrast in height. The key argument is that allomorphy preserves the contrast in height despite palatalization.

4.4.2 Allomorph distribution

In this section I further discuss allomorph distribution in the locative of masculine and neuter nouns in Polish. The allomorphs are in near complementary distribution. The front vowel allomorph [-e] also occurs after labials and labio-dentals *p*, *b*, *m*, *w*, *f*, *v*. The back vowel allomorph [-u] occurs in addition after post-alveolars *š*, *ž*, *č*, *dž*, the palatal *j*, velars *k*, *g*, *x*, alveolar affricates *c*, *dz*, and the lateral *l*. I will refer to those two groups as front and back consonants.[9]

(4-24) Front and back stems[10]

a. Front consonants (labials and labio-dentals)

		nominative sg.	**locative sg.**	**gloss**
p → p'j	:	chło[p]	o chło[p'] + je	'peasant'
b → b'j	:	ara[b]	o ara[b'] + je	'Arab'
m → m'j	:	gra[m]	o gra[m'] + je	'gram'
f → f'j	:	gra[f]	o gra[f'] + je	'graph'
v → v'j	:	ró[v]	o ro[v'] + je	'ditch'

b. Back consonants (post-alveolars, the palatal, velars, alveolar affricates, and the lateral)

		nominative sg.	locative sg.	gloss
š	:	ko[š]	o ko[š] + u	'basket'
ž	:	tale[ž]	o tale[ž] + u	'plate'
č	:	królewi[č]	o królewi[č] + u	'prince'
dž	:	bry[dž]	o bry[dž] + u	'bridge'
j	:	kra[j]	o kra[j] + u	'country'
k	:	so[k]	o so[k] + u	'juice'
g	:	ró[g]	o ro[g] + u	'corner, horn'
x	:	stra[x]	o stra[x] + u	'fear'
c	:	ko[c]	o ko[c] + u	'blanket'
dz	:	wi[dz]	o wi[dz] + u	'viewer'
l	:	nauczycie[l]	o nauczycie[l] + u	'teacher'

As shown above, consonants articulated in the front part of the oral cavity take the front vowel allomorph [-e] (see (4-24a)). Consonants articulated in the back part of the oral cavity take the back vowel allomorph [-u] (see (4-24b)).[11]

This is also true of borrowings. Front consonants take the [–e] suffix while back consonants take the [–u] suffix.

(4-25) Borrowings

nominative sg.	locative sg.	gloss
gadže[t]	o gadže[ć] + e	'gadget' (English)
Harwar[d]	o Harwar[dź] + e	'Harvard' (English)
autobu[s]	o autobu[ś] + e	'bus'
trape[z]	o trape[ź] + e	'trapèze' (French)
badminto[n]	o badminto[ń] + e	'badminton' (English)

nominative sg.	locative sg.	gloss
bry[dž]	o bry[dž] + u	'bridge' (English)
alkoho[l]	o alkoho[l] + u	'Alkohol' (German)
zam[š]	o zam[š] + u	'Sämisch' (German)
gara[ž]	o gara[ž] + u	'garage' (French)
Nowy Jor[k]	o Nowym Jor[k] + u	'New York'

As shown above, the allomorphs are in near complementary distribution. The front vowel allomorph is preferred for front consonants and the back allomorph is preferred for back consonants. To express this generalization, I will assume that [u] is preferred over [e] (*e >> *u) but not after front consonants (*Front/u >> *e). The constraint *Front/u is a member of the family of No Linkage constraints proposed in Ito *et al*. (1995). The constraints and their ranking are illustrated below.

(4-26) *Front/u

No back vowels after front consonants.

(4-27) Allomorph distribution
*Front/u >> *e >> *u

The ranking given in (4-27) is represented in the following tableaux. Tableau (4-28) represents a stem ending in a back consonant, a post-alveolar, and it selects the back vowel allomorph in the locative. Tableau (4-29) shows a stem ending in a front consonant, a labial, and it selects the front vowel allomorph in the locative.

(4-28) Back consonants select [-u]

	/talež, {+u, +e}/	*Front/u	*e	*u
☞	a. talež + u			*
	b. talež + e		*!	

(4-29) Front consonants select [-e][12]

	/graf, {+u, +e}/	*Front/u	*e	*u
	a. graf + u	*!		*
☞	b. graf' + je		*	

In effect, back consonants select the back allomorph (see (4-28)) while front consonants select the front allomorph (see (4-29)).

This preference is only active in allomorph selection. Both sequences surface when underlying. Kager (1996) refers to this type of markedness as morphological markedness in contrast to phonological markedness.

(4-30) Underlying sequences of Front/u
[du]x 'ghost'
[pu]zon 'trombone'
[nu]rek 'diver'
[su]peł 'knot'

To ensure that there are words in Polish with a front consonant followed by a back vowel, preserving the contrast in vowel quality, PC_{IN}(high)/PC_{IN}(back)/PC_{IN}(round), is more important than avoiding back vowels after front consonants, *Front/u. The constraints on preserving contrast in vowel quality are members of a family of PC constraints defined in section 4.3. They are formulated under the assumption that vowels in Polish can be defined in terms of height, backness, and rounding (Rubach 1984). The ranking is given below.

(4-31) PC_{IN}(high), PC_{IN}(back), PC_{IN}(round) >> *Front/u

I will compare two existing forms of Polish, [dux] 'ghost' vs. [dex] 'breath'. The relevant tableau is given below.

(4-32) Underlying Front/u sequences surface[13]

	Scenarios	PC_{IN}(high)	PC_{IN}(back)	PC_{IN}(round)	*Front/u
(i) Contrast-preserving ☞	/dux/ → dux /dex/ → dex				*
(ii) Contrast-neutralizing	/dux/ → dex /dex/ → dex	*	*	*!	

The constraints against neutralizing the contrast between vowels of different height, backness, and rounding select the scenario where the contrast is preserved, scenario (i). Scenario (ii) violates the PC constraints.[14]

This is an example of "the emergence of the unmarked" or TETU effects (Mascaró 1996, McCarthy and Prince 1995). The markedness constraints guiding allomorph selection are not otherwise active in the language since they are dominated by conflicting faithfulness (in my account, by PC constraints). For discussion of "the emergence of the unmarked" in allomorph selection, see Kager (1999b), McCarthy (2004), Wolf (2008), and references cited within.

4.4.3 The role of contrast

Given the palatalization facts and the articulation of prepalatals, I assume that prepalatals followed by [-e] are unmarked. The argument for this is two-fold. First, the sequence of a prepalatal followed by a front vowel is the output of palatalization. It has been shown that a phonological process in OT must lead to a decrease in markedness (see Moreton 1996/1999). In addition, prepalatals are articulatorily similar to a front vowel, as the tongue body in the articulation of prepalatals is moved forward (see Ladefoged and Maddieson 1996, Rubach 1984: 24). Because of the position of the tongue body, prepalatals are described as [–back]. Given this evidence, the allomorph [-u] after original prepalatals is unexpected. The tableaux below show that, under the constraint ranking established so far, both derived and underlying prepalatals should select the same allomorph.[15]

(4-33) Derived prepalatals

	/list, {+u, +e}/	*Front/u	*e	*u
	a. list + u	*!		*
☞	b. liść + e		*	

(4-34) Underlying prepalatals – wrong result

	/liść, {+u, +e}/	*Front/u	*e	*u
☜	a. liść + u	*!		*
	b. liść + e		*	

As shown above, while derived prepalatals select the unmarked allomorph (see (4-33)), underlying prepalatals present a problem (see (4-34)). The winning mapping /liść/ → [liść + e] is not the actual mapping in Polish.

To ensure that derived and original prepalatals select different allomorphs, the constraint on contrast must compel the marked allomorph. Formally, the constraint on preserving contrast in height, PC_{IN}(high), must outrank the markedness constraint against the marked allomorph, which in my analysis is *Front/u. This is illustrated below. The tableau compares two scenarios, a contrast-preserving scenario, scenario (i), and a contrast-neutralizing scenario, scenario (ii).

(4-35) The role of contrast

	Scenarios	PC_{IN}(high)	*Front/u
(i) Contrast-preserving ☞	/list, {+e, +u}/ → liść + e /liść, {+e, +u}/ → liść + u		*
(ii) Contrast-neutralizing	/list, (+e, +u}/ → liść + e /liść, {+e, +u}/ → liść + e	*!	

Scenario (i) wins since it preserves the contrast between derived and original prepalatals by the choice of a different allomorph. Stems that end in a prepalatal in the input as opposed to the ones where the prepalatal is derived select different allomorphs. Scenario (ii) loses since it neutralizes the contrast in height, even though it chooses the less marked allomorph. Thus, the marked allomorph retains the contrast between the two sets of prepalatals.

4.4.4 Summary

In summary, palatalization takes place but allomorphy preserves the contrast in height despite palatalization. Contrast preservation and the need to palatalize compel the marked allomorph after underlying prepalatals. This is illustrated in the following tableau.

(4-36) Summary tableau

	Scenarios	PAL	PC_{IN}(high)	*Front/u
(i) Contrast-neutralizing	/list, {+e, +u}/ → liść + e /liść, {+e, +u}/ → liść + e		*!	
(ii) Contrast-preserving ☞ (=Actual)	/list, {+e, +u}/ → liść + e /liść, {+e, +u}/ → liść + u			*
(iii) Contrast-preserving	/list, {+e, +u}/ → list + e /liść, {+e, +u}/ → liść + e	*!		

Scenario (ii) wins since it preserves the contrast in height and palatalizes. In terms of constraints, it satisfies both PAL and PC_{IN}(high). Scenario (i) loses since it neutralizes the contrast in height, thus violating PC_{IN}(high). Scenario (iii) loses since it fails to palatalize, thus violating PAL.

The ranking established so far is given below. This is followed by the ranking arguments.

(4-37) Ranking established so far

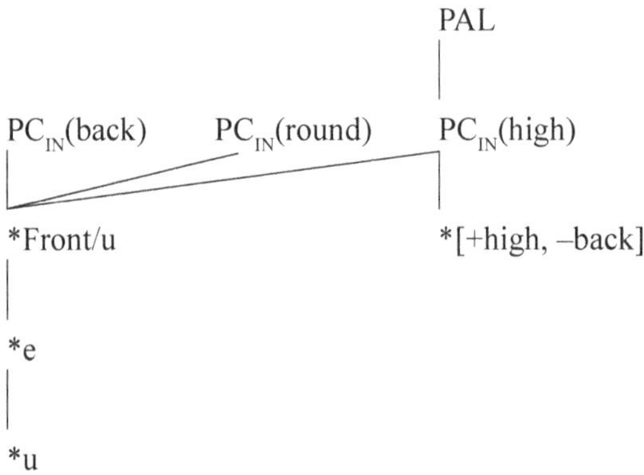

(4-38) Ranking arguments

Ranking	Argument
PAL >> PC_{IN}(high)	Palatalization neutralizes the height contrast.
PC_{IN}(high) >> *[+high, - back]	Underlying prepalatals are acceptable.
*Front/u >> *e >> *u	Allomorphs are in complementary distribution.
PC_{IN}(high) >> *Front/u	Contrast compels the marked allomorph.
PC_{IN}(back/round/high) >> *Front/u	Underlying Front/u sequences are acceptable.

The key idea is that with different allomorphs in the locative for derived and underlying prepalatals, palatalization is non-neutralizing. The contrast in height is preserved despite palatalization.

4.5 Predictions and comparison with previous approaches

In this section I discuss predictions of the contrast approach to allomorphy. I first discuss other logical scenarios in the Polish locative (4.5.1), and then compare the predictions of the contrast account with alternative approaches to allomorphy (4.5.2).

4.5.1 The typology

In PC theory, a candidate is a scenario. In the actual scenario, derived prepalatals take the [-e] allomorph while underlying prepalatals take the [-u] allomorph. But there are other scenarios that need to be considered. We need to ensure that under our analysis the actual scenario wins over other possibilities. Formally, considering the two inputs, /list/ vs. /liść/, and the two allomorphs {+e, +u}, there are 16 logical scenarios to consider. These are shown below. The actual scenario is number (i) and is represented in a bold box. I divide the scenarios into contrast-preserving and contrast-neutralizing.

(4-39) Logical scenarios

Contrast-preserving scenarios			
(i)	/list, {+e, +u}/ → liść + e /liść, {+e, +u}/ → liść + u	(ix)	/list, {+e, +u}/ → liść + u /liść, {+e, +u}/ → liść + e
(ii)	/list, {+e, +u}/ → list + u /liść, {+e, +u}/ → liść + e	(x)	/list, {+e, +u}/ → liść + e /liść, {+e, +u}/ → list + u
(iii)	/list, {+e, +u}/ → list + u /liść, {+e, +u}/ → liść+ u	(xi)	/list, {+e, +u}/ → liść + u /liść, {+e, +u}/ → list + u
(iv)	/list, {+e, +u}/ → list + e /liść, {+e, +u}/ → liść + e	(xii)	/list, {+e, +u}/ → liść + e /liść, {+e, +u}/ → list + e
(v)	/list, {+e, +u}/ → list + u /liść, {+e, +u}/ → list + e	(xiii)	/list, {+e, +u}/ → list + e /liść, {+e, +u}/ → list + u
(vi)	/list, {+e, +u}/ → list + e /liść, {+e, +u}/ → liść + u	(xiv)	/list, {+e, +u}/ → liść + u /liść, {+e, +u}/ → list + e
Contrast-neutralizing scenarios			
(vii)	/list, {+e, +u}/ → liść + e /liść, {+e, +u}/ → liść + e	(xv)	/list, {+e, +u}/ → list + e /liść, {+e, +u}/ → list + e
(viii)	/list, {+e, +u}/ → list + u /liść, {+e, +u}/ → list + u	(xvi)	/list, {+e, +u}/ → liść + u /liść, {+e, +u}/ → liść + u

The scenarios represent various mapping coexistence patterns. They have the same inputs but differ on the set of outputs (compare (i) and (vii)) and/or input–output relations (compare (i) and (ix)). Scenario (i) is the actual scenario in Polish where the two inputs take different allomorphs. Scenario (vii), on the other hand, represents a language where both inputs take the same allomorph [-e].[16]

Some scenarios are eliminated, given the constraint ranking established so far. Any scenario that does not palatalize is ruled out. This rules out scenarios (iv)–(vi) and (xii)–(xv). Also, any scenario that neutralizes the height contrast is ruled out. That rules out scenarios (vii), (viii), (xv), and (xvi). These are the shaded scenarios. We are left with six scenarios to consider. The remaining contrast-preserving scenarios are given below.

(4-40) Remaining contrast-preserving scenarios

(i) Actual	/list, {+e, +u}/ → liść + e /liść, {+e, +u}/ → liść + u	(ix)	/list, {+e, +u}/ → liść + u /liść, {+e, +u}/ → liść + e
(ii)	/list, {+e, +u}/ → list + u /liść, {+e, +u}/ → liść + e	(x)	/list, {+e, +u}/ → liść + e /liść, {+e, +u}/ → list + u
(iii)	/list, {+e, +u}/ → list + u /liść, {+e, +u}/ → liść + u	(xi)	/list, {+e, +u}/ → liść + u /liść , {+e, +u}/ → list + u

All the scenarios given above satisfy PAL and PC_{IN}(high). They differ, however, on how contrast is actually preserved.

Contrast-preserving scenarios (ii), (iii), (x), and (xi) differ from the actual scenario on the set of outputs. While the actual scenario contains a prepalatal followed by the back vowel [u], the other four scenarios contain an alveolar followed by [u]. It has been shown that allomorphs in the locative are distributed on the front-back dimension where front consonants take the front allomorph and back consonants take the back allomorph. This fact is expressed by a contextual markedness constraint *Front/u. The difference between the actual scenario and the other competing scenarios above argues that consonants which are classified as front, such as alveolars and prepalatals, need to be further differentiated. In this case, I propose that the contextual markedness constraint *Front/u is divided into *Alveolar/u and *Prepalatal/u, where *Alveolar/u dominates *Prepalatal/u. It is worse for the alveolar consonant to be followed by [u] than for the prepalatal. The alveolar is more front than the prepalatal and thus more different in place of articulation from the back vowel. The ranking is given below:

(4-41) The scale of "frontness"
*Alveolar/u >> *Prepalatal/u[17]

The consequence of this ranking is that the Alveolar/u sequence is less optimal than the sequence of Prepalatal/u. This is illustrated below. I compare the actual scenario to a competing scenario with a more marked output.

(4-42) The role for markedness

		PAL	PC_{IN}(high)	*Alveolar/u	*Prepalatal/u
(i) ☞	/list, {+e, +u}/ → liść + e /liść, {+e, +u}/ → liść + u				*
(ii)	/list, {+e, +u}/ → list + u /liść, {+e, +u}/ → liść + e			*!	

The actual scenario, scenario (i), wins since it contains a less marked output.

Let us now consider scenario (ix), which has the same set of outputs as the optimal scenario but the outputs are permuted. The permuted scenario is recalled below. It is represented alongside the actual scenario.

(4-43) Permuted scenario
/list, {+e, +u}/ → liść + u
/liść , {+e, +u}/ → liść + e

(4-44) Actual scenario
/list, {+e, +u}/ → liść + e
/liść , {+e, +u}/ → liść + u

Both scenarios satisfy markedness and contrast equally. They have the same outputs but these outputs correspond to different inputs. In terms of constraints, there is a tie between the permuted scenario and the actual scenario. The tie is represented in the following tableau.

(4-45) A tie between scenarios

	Scenarios	PAL	PC_{IN}(high)	*Front/u
(i) Permuted	/list, {+e, +u}/ → liść + u /liść, {+e, +u}/ → liść + e			*
(ii) Actual	/list, {+e, +u}/ → liść + e /liść, {+e, +u}/ → liść + u			*

Both candidates satisfy PAL and PC_{IN}(high). They also both incur a violation of *Front/u since they each contain an output where a prepalatal consonant is followed by the back vowel.

The constraint on recoverability introduced in Chapter 3 (section 3.4.1) breaks the tie between the two scenarios. Such a constraint demands that the input contrast in P be retained in the output in the same direction as in the input (see (3-19)). In Polish, this constraint requires that the higher the stem-final consonant, the higher the suffix. The input height contrast needs to be read off from the output distribution of the allomorphs. As explained in Chapter 3, recoverability constraints belong to the second stage of Eval after PC and markedness apply.

(4-46) Recover (high) (cf. (3-19) and (3-20))
Let a pair of inputs in_a and in_b minimally contrast in [+/−high] and corresponding outputs minimally contrast in u~e, if in_a is [+high] and in_b is [−high], then out_a has [−u] and out_b has [−e].
"The minimal input contrast in height needs to be preserved in the output in the same direction."

(4-47) The role of Recover

		PAL	PC_{IN}(high)	*Alv/u	*Prepal/u	Recover (high)
(i) ☞	/list, {+e, +u}/ → liść + e /liść, {+e, +u}/ → liść + u				*	
(ii)	/list, {+e, +u}/ → liść + u /liść, {+e, +u}/ → liść + e				*	*!

Scenario (ii) loses since in this scenario the height contrast is permuted.

Recoverability captures the observation that in Polish the choice of the suffix [–e] vs. [–u] signals the quality of the stem-final consonant in the input. The original contrast in height is preserved but displaced from its original position and realized by the suffix.[18]

As discussed in Chapter 3, this has parallels to a feature movement approach where the relevant feature is preserved from the input in the output but displaced from its original position. Feature movement is traditionally captured with MAX(feature) constraints (Lombardi 2001). In a feature movement approach, contrast can only be preserved by the same feature as in the input while in a contrast-preservation account other representations of contrast are possible.[19] The properties evaluated by recoverability are determined in stage 1 of Eval.

The ranking is summarized below.

(4-48) Full ranking

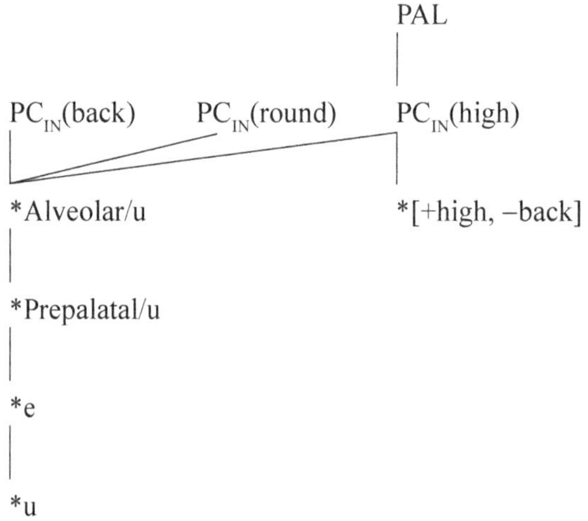

PAL

PC_{IN}(back) PC_{IN}(round) PC_{IN}(high)

*Alveolar/u *[+high, –back]

*Prepalatal/u

*e

*u

Second stage of Eval: RECOVER(high)

Harmonically bounded scenarios in Polish are discussed in the Appendix (A.2).

Under this proposal, allomorph distribution follows from the principle of contrast and morphological markedness. The constraint on contrast, PC_{IN}(high), together with a markedness constraint, PAL, force original prepalatals to take a different allomorph than underlying prepalatals. In consequence, allomorphy retains distinctions that would otherwise be neutralized in the output.

4.5.2 Comparison with previous approaches

In the account of allomorphy formulated in this chapter, contrast in addition to markedness determines allomorph distribution. Thus, in PC theory, the constraint on preserving contrast between dentals/alveolars vs. prepalatals, PC_{IN}(high), together with the constraint that results in palatalization, PAL, provide an explanation for allomorph distribution. Through the use of contrast as an imperative in a phonological system, PC theory predicts the kinds of allomorphy that are not admitted by other approaches. In what follows, I will compare the predictions of PC theory to markedness-only approaches to allomorphy and to subcategorization approaches.

In markedness-only approaches (see the references in section 4.4.1), allomorphs are distributed based on the properties of the output alone. Thus, output well-formedness is the only criterion by which allomorph distribution is determined. In terms of constraints, allomorph distribution is accounted for only by markedness constraints. As was explained in the introduction, markedness-only approaches fail to explain allomorphy that is determined by factors other than output well-formedness. Unlike markedness-only approaches, in PC theory, contrast in addition to markedness determines allomorph distribution. Thus, PC theory admits cases of opaque allomorphy which cannot be accounted for in markedness-only terms. Polish locative is an example of this kind of allomorphy. In addition, PC theory predicts the kinds of allomorphy that are predicted by markedness-only approaches since markedness is also present in allomorph selection in this framework.

In a subcategorization approach (Booij and Lieber 1993, Paster 2005), allomorph distribution is accounted for by rules that refer to the properties of the input. This is a very different approach from the research program developed in this chapter. In a subcategorization approach, there are no limits on what rules are possible and thus there are no limits on what kinds of allomorphy are possible. Unlike the subcategorization approach, PC theory developed in this chapter is significantly more restrictive. In PC, there are restrictions on the possible distribution of allomorphs since these patterns should fall out from universal constraints on markedness and contrast.

In summary, PC theory can compel allomorphy in cases where allomorphy is unexpected based on the well-formedness of the output (as in markedness-only approaches) or based on the properties of the input (as in the subcategorization approach).[20] Finally, PC theory gives an account of opaque allomorphy within the framework of parallel OT. No special mechanism is required to account for opaque allomorphy since in this approach contrast is an inherent property of the grammar.

4.6 Conclusion

In this chapter, I have accounted for Polish allomorphy in the locative of masculine and neuter nouns. I have shown that locative allomorph distribution is opaque and can be accounted for in terms of preserving contrast.

A formal account of contrast preservation in the case of affix allomorphy has been proposed. The key idea is that the different allomorphs of the locative suffix keep apart forms that the regular phonology would otherwise neutralize. Under this proposal, allomorph distribution follows from the principle of contrast and markedness. The PC account has been shown to admit the kinds of allomorphy that are not predicted by previous approaches.

Notes

1. For non-OT accounts of allomorphy, see Carstairs-McCarthy (1988), Hudson (1974), and Siegel (1974). For a more complete list of references, see McCarthy (2004).
2. The terms "morphological opacity" and "opaque allomorphy" are used interchangeably.
3. In this chapter, I will follow Rubach's (1984) description of Polish and use the following transcription system: *c* – voiceless alveolar affricate, *dz* – voiced alveolar affricate, *š* –voiceless postalveolar fricative, *ž* – voiced postalveolar fricative, č – voiceless postalveolar affricate, *dž* – voiced postalveolar affricate, *ś* – voiceless prepalatal fricative, *ź* – voiced prepalatal fricative, *ć* – voiceless prepalatal affricate, *dź* – voiced prepalatal affricate, and *ń* –prepalatal nasal. The examples are from both Rubach (1984) and the author who is a native speaker of Polish.
4. There are two other mappings that undergo coronal palatalization: r → ž (rowe[r] ~ o rowe[ž] + e 'bicycle'), and w → l (ko[w] + o ~ o ko[l] + e 'circle'). In both cases, the locative suffix is [-e], whereas the same segments present underlyingly take the [-u] suffix, e.g. ryce[ž] ~ ryce[ž]+u 'knight', and po[l]+e ~ po[l]+u 'field'.
5. A more precise formulation given in Rubach (1984) is: [+anter, +coron, -del rel, α obstr] → [–back, +distr, +high, –anter, α strid] / ______ [–cons, –back]. This excludes alveolar affricates and the lateral [l] from the input to palatalization. Two other mappings that undergo coronal palatalization but are not discussed here are: /w r/ → [l ž].
6. The sounds also differ in [+/- anterior].
7. Other scenarios in the same candidate set are discussed in section 4.5.
8. This needs to be decided in round one, with PC(high) rather than later by IO-Faith. There are no markedness constraints in stage 2 of Eval.
9. This corresponds to Rubach's (1984) classification as [+anterior] for front consonants and [–anterior] for back consonants. The only exceptions are *c*, *dz*, and *l* that are [+anterior] but pattern with back consonants. There is evidence from Polish that *c*, *dz* pattern together with post-alveolars. For example, both condition the process of vowel retraction. The patterning of *l* with [–anterior] might have to do with historical dark *l*.
10. Two other palatalizations are shown in (4-24a): labio-velar palatalization and surface palatalization. Following Rubach (1984), labio-velar palatalization is formulated as: ∅ → j / [–coronal] ____ e. Surface palatalization is formulated as: [+cons] → [+high, –back] / ____ ([–seg]) [–cons, +high, –back]. Exceptions include masculine nouns that end in a bilabial or alveolar but can take either the [–u] ending: do[m] – o do[m] + u, sy[n] – o sy[n] + u, or the front [–e] ending. There are also a few masculine nouns that pattern as feminine in the locative (not discussed here).
11. Diachronically, it has been argued that Polish allomorphy in the locative follows a distribution where the so-called u-stems in Early Slavic take the [–u] ending and the so-called o-stems take the [–e] ending (Lunt 2001, Szober 1969). It is also described in terms of hard and soft stems, where stems ending in soft consonants take the [–u] ending. The term "soft" indicates consonants that are synchronically soft, such as prepalatals, or used to be soft, such as post-alveolars. The latter is referred to as "functionally soft" (Jaworski 1986, Szober 1969). Stems ending in hard consonants take the [–e] ending.

12. As described in footnote 10, the presence of "j" in candidate (b) is due to a regular phonological process in Polish, called labio-velar palatalization (see Rubach 1984).
13. The tableau only illustrates the need for one of the PC_{IN} constraints. The reason why all three PC_{IN} constraints need to be ranked above *Front/u is to prevent across-the-board neutralizations in vowel quality in order to avoid Front/u sequences.
14. A permuted scenario where the outputs are the same as in the actual scenario but they correspond to different inputs is discussed in section 4.4.5.
15. "Front" in my account includes prepalatals.
16. Some of the logically possible scenarios represented in (4-39) are harmonically bounded and will never win given the constraint inventory postulated in this work (see the Appendix, A-2).
17. An alternative would be to have a specific constraint *Alveolar/u outranking *Front/u.
18. To answer a reviewer's question, if the allomorphs in Polish preserving the contrast between alveolars/prepalatals were e/o, the relevant RECOVER constraint would need to refer to a property in the alveolar/prepalatal contrast that is related to the e/o contrast, for example [+/–anterior]. The constraint would say "If in–1 is [+anterior] and in–2 is [–anterior], then out–1 has [–e] and out–2 has [–o]."
19. Thanks to Maria Gouskova for bringing up this point.
20. PC theory can also block allomorphy in cases where allomorphy is expected based on the well-formedness of the output (as in markedness-only approaches) or based on the properties of the input (as in the subcategorization approach).

5 Conclusion

This chapter summarizes the results of this work and deals with any remaining questions. This book has argued that contrast is one of the central organizing principles of the grammar and developed an Optimality-Theoretic framework for contrast called PC ("preserve contrast") theory.

The key idea is that chain shifts and other opaque morphophonological processes involve *contrast transformation* where a given underlying contrast is manifested as a different surface contrast. This is at the cost of neutralizing some other contrast in the system. PC theory provides a formal way to account for contrast transformation.

The core of the proposal is that there exists a family of rankable and violable anti-neutralization constraints on preserving contrasts, called PC constraints. Such constraints interact with one another and with conflicting markedness constraints resulting in preservation and/or neutralization of contrasts. There are also generalized faithfulness constraints in the theory to resolve ties among candidates (Chapter 2). Generalized faithfulness constraints are formulated as recoverability in Chapters 3 and 4. Constraints belong to two stages of Eval. PC constraints and markedness are in stage 1 while generalized faithfulness constraints are in stage 2.

In this proposal, contrast is evaluated over a finite set of input–output mappings, called a scenario. An algorithm for scenario construction was given in Chapter 2. Scenarios represent various mapping interactions and the optimal scenario is chosen by the rankable and violable constraints.

PC theory was introduced on the example of chain shift mappings in Chapter 2 and further motivated with the examples of phonological and morphological contrasts in Chapters 3 and 4. Chapter 2 discussed the typology of chain shift mappings predicted by PC theory. The main implication is that PC theory allows for push shift mappings which are not admitted under previous approaches. Chapter 3 took a look at the typology of stress-epenthesis interaction and showed that PC theory makes accurate predictions as to what types of systems are generated in the grammar. For example, it predicts that there occur hybrid dialects in addition to contrast-preserving and contrast-neutralizing dialects. It also predicts that onset dialects are never contrast-preserving. This chapter also discussed locality of contrast transformation. Finally, Chapter 4 considered ways in which PC theory can be extended to explain cases of morphological contrast using the example of opaque allomorphy. Allomorphy would usually be treated in a different way from chain shifts or stress-epenthesis interaction while PC theory provides a way to unify what previously seemed like separate phenomena.

PC theory has far-reaching consequences for our understanding of the workings of a phonological system. It proposes that constraints on contrast are a formal part of the grammar rather than a derivative in a phonological system as in previous approaches. One of the key implications of this proposal is that contrast together with markedness can trigger a phonological process. This makes different predictions from previous approaches as to what phonological mappings are possible. Furthermore, PC theory provides a uniform way to account for transparent and opaque phonological processes with no additional mechanisms required.

It is my hope that this book has provided a formal way to discuss contrast in phonology and morphophonology and has opened many avenues for further research.

Appendix

A.1 Constraint violations in Finnish

This section provides a summary tableau for constraint violations in Finnish. The constraints are unranked. Harmonically bounded scenarios are shaded.

Let us look at constraint violations. Input-oriented PC constraints, PC_{IN}(long) and PC_{IN}(round), are violated by all scenarios in which there are input pairs distinct in length or rounding that map onto the same output. PC_{IN}(long) is violated in all scenarios but the bi-directional scenarios (iv) and (v). PC_{IN}(round) is violated in all scenarios but the transparent scenario (i) and a multi-directional scenario (xiv). Output-oriented PC constraints, PC_{OUT}(round) and PC_{OUT}(long), are violated by the same scenarios as input-oriented PC constraints along the same dimensions. The difference lies in how neutralizations are distributed among outputs. In comparison to the transparent scenarios (ii) and (iii), the opaque scenarios (ix) through (xii) incur fewer violations of PC_{OUT}(long). The relational PC constraint, PC_{REL}(rd), is violated by the bi-directional scenarios (iv) and (v) because in those scenarios input–output contrasts undergo absolute neutralization. Furthermore, tokenized markedness *ai and *oi distinguishes between scenarios that involve rounding versus lowering: total merger scenarios (ii) and (iii), chain shifts (ix) and (x), and derived environment effects (xi) and (xii). Finally, generalized faithfulness (–rd)–FAITH and (+rd)–FAITH distinguishes between scenarios with a different degree of input–output disparity (chain shifts versus derived environment effects (ix) vs. (xi) and (x) vs. (xii), bi-directional scenarios (iv) vs. (v)), and harmonically binds scenarios that involve unnecessary movement.

(A-1) Constraint violations

Scenarios	$*\sigma_{\mu\mu\mu}$	PC_{REL} (rd)	PC_{OUT} (long)	PC_{IN} (long)	PC_{OUT} (rd)	PC_{IN} (rd)	*ai	*oi	(-rd)-FAITH	(+rd)-FAITH
(i) Transparent			**	**			**	**	*	*
(ii) Total merger			*	****	*	****		****		****
(iii) Total merger (reverse)			*	****	*	****	****		****	
(iv) Bi-directional		*			**	**	**	**	***	*
(v) Bi-directional (reverse)		*			**	**	**	**	*	***
(vi) Cross-corner			**	**	**	**	**	**	**	**
(vii) Cross-corner			*	**	*	**	***	*	***	**
(viii) Cross-corner			*	**	*	**	*	***	**	***
(ix) CHS			*	**	*	**	*	***	*	**
(x) CHS (reverse)			*	**	*	**	***	*	**	*
(xi) DEE			*	**	*	**	*	***		***
(xii) DEE (reverse)			*	**	*	**	***	*	***	
(xiii) Multi-directional			**	**	**	**	**	**	**	**
(xiv) Multi-directional			**	**			**	**	***	***
(xv) Multi-directional			*	**	*	**	*	***	*	****
(xvi) Multi-directional			*	**	*	**	***	*	****	*

A.2 Harmonic bounding in Polish

This section illustrates harmonic bounding in Polish. Many of the logically possible scenarios represented in (4-39) are harmonically bounded. Following the representation in Chapter 2, harmonically bounded scenarios are shaded in the table below.

(A-2) Harmonic bounding (cf. 4-39)

Contrast-preserving scenarios			
(i)	/list, {+e, +u}/ → liść + e /liść, {+e, +u}/ → liść + u	(ix)	/list, {+e, +u}/ → liść + u /liść, {+e, +u}/ → liść + e
(ii)	/list, {+e, +u}/ → list + u /liść, {+e, +u}/ → liść + e	(x)	/list, {+e, +u}/ → liść + e /liść, {+e, +u}/ → list + u
(iii)	/list, {+e, +u}/ → list + u /liść, {+e, +u}/ → liść + u	(xi)	/list, {+e, +u}/ → liść + u /liść, {+e, +u}/ → list + u
(iv)	/list, {+e, +u}/ → list + e /liść, {+e, +u}/ → liść + e	(xii)	/list, {+e, +u}/ → liść + e /liść, {+e, +u}/ → list + e
(v)	/list, {+e, +u}/ → list + u /liść, {+e, +u}/ → list + e	(xiii)	/list, {+e, +u}/ → list + e /liść , {+e, +u}/ → list + u
(vi)	/list, {+e, +u}/ → list + e /liść , {+e, +u}/ → liść + u	(xiv)	/list, {+e, +u}/ → liść + u /liść, {+e, +u}/ → list + e
Contrast-neutralizing scenarios			
(vii)	/list, {+e, +u}/ → liść + e /liść, {+e, +u}/ → liść + e	(xv)	/list, {+e, +u}/ → list + e /liść, {+e, +u}/ → list + e
(viii)	/list, {+e, +u}/ → list + u /liść, {+e, +u}/ → list + u	(xvi)	/list, {+e, +u}/ → liść + u /liść, {+e, +u}/ → liść + u

Most of the scenarios are harmonically bounded in Stage 1 of Eval. Scenarios (vi) and (xiv) are harmonically bounded by scenario (i) by markedness (see (A-3)).

(A-3)

Scenarios	PAL	PC_{IN}(high)	*Alv/u	*Prepal/u	*e	*u
(i)				*	*	*
(vi)	*			*	*	*
(xiv)	*			*	*	*

Scenario (xv) is harmonically bounded by scenario (iv) by contrast and markedness (see (A-4)).

(A-4)

Scenarios	PAL	PC_{IN}(high)	*Alv/u	*Prepal/u	*e	*u
(iv)	*				**	
(xv)	**	*			**	

Given fixed ranking of contraints on allomorph selection, (a) scenarios (ii), (iii), (x), and (xi) are harmonically bounded by scenario (i) (see (A-5)), (b) scenarios (v) and (xiii) are harmonically bounded by scenario (iv) (see (A-6)), and (c) scenarios (viii) and (xvi) are harmonically bounded by scenario (vii) (see (A-7)).

(A-5)

Scenarios	PAL	PC_{IN}(high)	*Alv/u	*Prepal/u	*e	*u
(i)				*	*	*
(ii)			*		*	*
(iii)			*	*		**
(x)			*		*	*
(xi)			*	*		**

(A-6)

Scenarios	PAL	PC_{IN}(high)	*Alv/u	*Prepal/u	*e	*u
(iv)	*				**	
(v)	*		*		*	*
(xiii)	*		*		*	*

(A-7)

Scenarios	PAL	PC_{IN}(high)	*Alv/u	*Prepal/u	*e	*u
(vii)		*			**	
(viii)		*	**			**
(xvi)		*		**		**

Two other scenarios are harmonically bounded in Stage 2 of Eval on recoverability and generalized faithfulness: scenario (ix) is harmonically bounded by scenario (i) (see (A-8)), and scenario (xii) is harmonically bounded by scenario (iv) (see (A-9)).

(A-8)

Scenarios	PAL	PC_{IN}(high)	*Alv/u	*Prepal/u	*e	*u	RECOVER (high)
(i)				*	*	*	
(ix)				*	*	*	*

(A-9)

Scenarios	PAL	PC_{IN}(high)	*Alv/u	*Prepal/u	*e	*u	FAITH
(iv)	*				**		
(xii)	*				**		**

In summary, given the constraint inventory in Polish three scenarios are predicted to occur. These are the opaque allomorphy scenario (scenario (i)), the transparent scenario in which palatalization applies across the board (scenario (vii)), and the scenario in which palatalization underapplies (scenario (iv)). All are attested cross-linguistically as far as I know.

Bibliography

Abbreviations:

BLS	=	(Proceedings of the) Berkeley Linguistics Society
CLS	=	(Proceedings of the) Chicago Linguistics Society
LI	=	Linguistic Inquiry
NELS	=	(Proceedings of the) Northeast Linguistics Society
NLLT	=	Natural Language and Linguistic Theory
ROA	=	Rutgers Optimality Archive (http://ruccs.rutgers.edu/roa.html)
WCCFL	=	(Proceedings of the) West Coast Conference on Formal Linguistics

Abu-Mansour, Mahasen (1987) *A Nonlinear Analysis of Arabic Syllabic Phonology with Special Reference to Makkan.* Doctoral dissertation: University of Florida, Gainesville.

Ahn, Sang-Cheol (2004) Towards the Optimal Account of Diachronic Chain Shifts. *Studies in Phonetics, Phonology and Morphology* 10.1: 43–67.

Albright, Adam (2003) A Quantitative Study of Spanish Paradigm Gaps. In G. Garding and M. Tsujimura (eds) *WCCFL* 22: 1–14. Somerville, MA: Cascadilla Press.

Alderete, John (1995) Faithfulness to Prosodic Heads. Ms., University of Massachusetts, Amherst. [Available on Rutgers Optimality Archive, ROA-94.]

Alderete, John (1999) Head Dependence in Stress-Epenthesis Interaction. In Ben Hermans and Marc van Oostendorp (eds) *The Derivational Residue* 29–50. Amsterdam: John Benjamins. [Reprinted in *Optimality Theory in Phonology: Selected Readings* (2004), John McCarthy (ed), 215–27. Oxford: Blackwell.]

Alderete, John (2001a) *Morphologically Governed Accent in Optimality Theory.* New York and London: Routledge. [1999 Doctoral dissertation, University of Massachusetts, Amherst. Available on Rutgers Optimality Archive, ROA-309.]

Alderete, John (2001b) Dominance Effects as Transderivational Anti-faithfulness. *Phonology* 18: 201–53.

Anderson, Stephen R. and Browne, Wayles (1973) On Keeping Exchange Rules in Czech. *Papers in Linguistics* 6: 445–82.

Anttila, Arto (1995) Deriving Variation from Grammar: A Study of Finnish Genitives. Ms., Stanford University. [Available on Rutgers Optimality Archive, ROA-63.]

Anttila, Arto (1997) *Variation in Finnish Phonology and Morphology*. Doctoral dissertation: Stanford University.

Anttila, Arto (2000) Morphologically-Conditioned Phonological Alternations. Ms., Boston University and National University of Singapore.

Anttila, Arto (2002) Variation and Phonological Theory. In *The Handbook of Language Variation and Change*, 206–43. Oxford: Blackwell.

Apoussidou, Diana and Boersma, Paul (2004) Comparing Two Optimality-Theoretic Learning Algorithms for Latin Stress. *WCCFL* 23: 101–14. [ROA- 746]

Archangeli, Diana (1984) *Underspecification in Yawelmani Phonology and Morphology.* Doctoral dissertation: Massachusetts Institute of Technology. [Published 1988, Outstanding Dissertations in Linguistics Series, Garland, New York.]

Archangeli, Diana (1988) Aspects of Underspecification Theory. *Phonology* 5: 183–208.
Archangeli, Diana and Pulleyblank, Douglas (1994) *Grounded Phonology*. Cambridge, MA: MIT Press.
Avery, Peter, Dresher, B. Elan, and Rice, Keren (eds) (2008) *Contrast in Phonology: Theory, Perception, Acquisition*. Berlin: Mouton de Gruyter.
Barrie, Michael (2006) Tone Circles and Contrast Preservation. *LI* 37(1): 131–41.
Bauer, L. (1979) The Second Great Vowel Shift? *Journal of the International Phonetic Association* 9: 57–66.
Bauer, L. (1992) The Second Great Vowel Shift Revisited. *English World-Wide* 18: 253–68.
Benediktsson, Hreinn (ed.) (1970) *The Nordic Languages and Modern Linguistics*. Reykjavík: Societas Scientarium Islandica.
Benua, Laura (1997) *Transderivational Identity: Phonological Relations between Words*. Doctoral dissertation. Amherst, MA: University of Massachusetts, Amherst. [Available on Rutgers Optimality Archive, ROA-259. Published in (2000) as *Phonological Relations Between Words*, New York: Garland.]
Bermúdez-Otero, Ricardo (2007) Morphological Structure and Phonological Domains in Spanish Denominal Derivations. In Sonia Colina and Fernando Martinez-Gil (eds) *Optimality-theoretic Studies in Spanish Phonology*. Amsterdam: John Benjamins.
Bloomfield, Leonard (1984) *Language*. Chicago, IL: University of Chicago Press. [1933]
Bonet, Eulàlia (2004) Morph Insertion and Allomorphy in Optimality Theory. *International Journal of English Studies* 4: 73–104. Murcia, Spain: Universidad de Murcia.
Booij, G. and Lieber, R. (1993) On the Simultaneity of Morphological and Prosodic Structure. In S. Hargus and E. Kaisse (eds) *Studies in Lexical Phonology*, 23–44. San Diego, CA: Academic Press.
Borowsky, Toni (1986) *Topics in the Lexical Phonology of English*. Doctoral dissertation. Amherst, MA: University of Massachusetts, Amherst.
Bradley, Travis (2001) *The Phonetics and Phonology of Rhotic Duration Contrast and Neutralization*. Doctoral dissertation: University of California, Davis. [Available on Rutgers Optimality Archive, ROA-473.]
Bradley, Travis (2006) Contrast and Markedness in Complex Onset Phonotactics. *Journal of Southwest Linguistics* 25: 29–58.
Bradshaw, Mary (1996) One-Step Raising in Gbanu. In D. Dowty, R. Herman, E. Hume, and P. Pappas (eds) *Ohio State Working Papers in Linguistics* 48: 1–11.
Broselow, Ellen (1976) *The Phonology of Egyptian Arabic*. Doctoral dissertation. Amherst, MA: University of Massachusetts, Amherst.
Broselow, Ellen (1982) On Predicting the Interaction of Stress and Epenthesis. *Glossa* 16: 115–32.
Broselow, Ellen (1992) Parametric Variation in Arabic Dialect Phonology. In E. Broselow, M. Eid, and J. McCarthy (eds) *Perspectives on Arabic Linguistics* vol. 4: 7–45. Amsterdam and Philadelphia, PA: John Benjamins.
Broselow, Ellen (2001) Stress-Epenthesis Interactions. [ROA-466]
Broselow, Ellen, Chen, Su-I, and Huffman, Marie (1997) Syllable Weight: Convergence of Phonology and Phonetics. *Phonology* 14: 47–82.
Browman, Catherine and Goldstein, Louis (1986) Towards an Articulatory Phonology. *Phonology* 3: 219–52.
Burzio, Luigi (1996) Surface Constraints versus Underlying Representations. In J. Durand and B. Laks (eds) *Current Trends in Phonology: Models and Methods*, 123–42. Salford: European Studies Research Institute, University of Salford Publications.
Burzio, Luigi (1998) Multiple Correspondence. *Lingua* 103: 79–109.

Carstairs-McCarthy, Andrew (1988) Some Implications of Phonologically Conditioned Suppletion. *Yearbook of Morphology* 1988: 67–94. Dordrecht: Foris Publications.

Casenhiser, Devin (2005) Children's Resistance to Homonymy: An Experimental Study of Pseudohomonyms. *Journal of Child Language* 32.2: 319–43.

Ćavar, Malgorzata E. (2004) *Palatalization in Polish: An Interaction of Articulatory and Perceptual Factors*. Doctoral dissertation: University of Potsdam.

Chen, Matthew (1987) The Syntax of Xiamen Tone Sandhi. *Phonology Yearbook* 4: 107–49. Cambridge: Cambridge University Press.

Chomsky, Noam, and Halle, Morris (1968) *The Sound Pattern of English.* New York: Harper and Row. [Reprinted 1991, Boston, MA: MIT Press.]

Clements, George N. (1991) Vowel Height Assimilation in Bantu Languages. *BLS* 17: 25–63. Berkeley, CA: University of California.

Cote, Marie-Helene (2000) *Consonant Cluster Phonotactics: A Perceptual Approach.* Doctoral dissertation: Massachusetts Institute of Technology. [Available on Rutgers Optimality Archive, ROA-584.]

Cowell, Mark W. (1964) *A Reference Grammar of Syrian Arabic.* Washington, DC: Georgetown University Press.

Crosswhite, Katherine (1997/1999) Intra-paradigmatic Homophony Avoidance in Two Dialects of Slavic. Ms., University of California, Los Angeles.

Davis, Stuart (1995) Emphasis Spread in Arabic and Grounded Phonology. *LI* 26: 467–98.

Dinnsen, D. A. and Barlow, J. A. (1998) On the Characterization of a Chain Shift in Normal and Delayed Phonological Acquisition. *Journal of Child Language* 25: 61–94.

Donegan, Patricia J. and Stampe, David (1979) The Study of Natural Phonology. In Daniel A. Dinnsen (ed.) *Current Approaches to Phonological Theory*, 126–73. Bloomington, IN: Indiana University Press.

Downing, Laura J., Hall, T. A., and Raffelsiefen, Renate (eds) (2005) *Paradigms in Phonological Theory*. Oxford Studies in Theoretical Linguistics 8. Oxford: Oxford University Press.

Drachman G., Kager, R., and Malikouti-Drachman, A. (1995) Greek Allomorphy: an Optimality Account. In M. Dimitrova-Vulchanova and L. Hellan (eds) *Papers from the First Conference on Formal Approaches to South Slavic Languages*, 345–61. Plodiv, October 1995.

Dresher, B. Elan (2003) The Contrastive Hierarchy in Phonology. *Toronto Working Papers in Linguistics (Special Issue on Contrast in Phonology)* 20: 47–62.

Dresher, B. Elan, Piggott, Glyne, and Rice, Keren (1994) Contrast in Phonology: Overview. In C. Dyck (ed.) *Toronto Working Papers in Linguistics* 13.1: iii–xvii.

Erwin, Wallace M. (1963) *A Short Reference Grammar of Iraqi Arabic.* Washington, DC: Georgetown University Press.

Farwaneh, Samira (1995) *Directionality Effects in Arabic Dialect Syllable Structure.* Doctoral dissertation: University of Utah.

Feldstein, Ronald and Franks, Steven (2002) *Polish.* Munich: LINCOM Europa.

Firth, John Rupert (1957) *Papers in Linguistics 1934–1951*. London: Oxford University Press.

Fisher, W. M. and Hirsh, I. J. (1976) Intervocalic Flapping in English. *CLS* 12: 183–98.

Flack, Kathryn (2007) Ambiguity Avoidance as Contrast Preservation: Case and Word Order Freezing in Japanese. In L. Bateman, A. Werle, M. O'Keefe, and E. Reilly (eds) *UMass Occasional Papers in Linguistics 32: Papers in Optimality Theory III*: 57–88. [A longer version of this paper is available on ROA-748.]

Flemming, Edward (1995) *Auditory Representations in Phonology*. Doctoral dissertation: University of California, Los Angeles.

Flemming, Edward (1996) Evidence for Constraints on Contrast: The Dispersion Theory of Contrast. In Chai-Shune Hsu (ed.) *UCLA Working Papers in Phonology* 1: 86–106.

Flemming, Edward (2003) The Relationship between Coronal Place and Vowel Backness. *Phonology* 20: 335–72.

Flemming, Edward (2004) Contrast and Perceptual Distinctness. In B. Hayes, R. Kirchner, and D. Steriade (eds) *Phonetically-Based Phonology*, 232–76. Cambridge: Cambridge University Press.

Gafos, Adamantios (2002) A Grammar of Gestural Coordination. *NLLT* 20: 269–337.

Gafos, Diamandis and Ralli, A. (2002) Morphosyntactic Features and Paradigmatic Uniformity in Two Dialectal Varieties of the Island of Lesvos. *Journal of Greek Linguistics* 2: 41–73.

Gnanadesikan, Amalia E. (1997) *Phonology with Ternary Scales*. Doctoral dissertation. Amherst, MA: University of Massachusetts, Amherst.

Goldrick, Matthew and Smolensky, Paul (1999) Opacity and Turbid Representations in Optimality Theory. Talk presented at the CLS, April, 1999.

Gordon, E., Campbell, L., Hay, J., Maclagan, M., Sudbury, A., and Trudgill, P. (2004) *New Zealand English: Its Origins and Evolution.* Cambridge: Cambridge University Press.

Gordon, Matthew (2002) Weight-by-positon Adjunction and Syllable Structure. *Lingua* 112: 901–31.

Gouskova, Maria (2004) Minimal Reduplication as a Paradigm Uniformity Effect. In B. Schmeiser, V. Chand, A. Kelleher, and A. Rodriguez (eds) *WCCFL* 22: 265–78. Somerville, MA: Cscadilla Press.

Grzegorczykowa, Renata, Laskowski, Roman, and Wróbel, Henryk (eds) (1984) Gramatyka Współczesnego Języka Polskiego: Morfologia. Warszawa: PAN.

Gussmann, Edmund (1976) Recoverable Derivations and Phonological Change. *Lingua* 40: 281–303.

Gussmann, Edmund (1980) *Studies in Abstract Phonology*. Cambridge, MA: MIT Press.

Hall, Nancy (2003) *Gestures and Segments: Vowel Intrusion as Overlap*. Doctoral dissertation. Amherst, MA: University of Massachusetts, Amherst. [Available on Rutgers Optimality Archive, ROA-637.]

Halle, Morris and Vergnaud, Jean-Roger (1987) *An Essay on Stress*. Cambridge, MA: MIT Press.

Hamid, Abdel Halim (1984) *A Descriptive Analysis of Sudanese Colloquial Arabic Phonology*. Doctoral dissertation: University of Illinois, Urbana-Champaign.

Hargus, Sharon and Tuttle, Siri G. (1997) Augmentation as Affixation in Athabaskan Languages. *Phonology* 14: 177–220.

Harrell, Richard S. (1957) *The Phonology of Colloquial Egyptian Arabic*. New York: American Council of Learned Societies.

Harrikari, Heli (1999) Inalterability of Long Vowels in Finnish. Handout from Rutgers/UMass Joint Class Meeting.

Harrikari, Heli (2000) *Segmental Length in Finnish – Studies within a Constraint-based Approach*. Doctoral dissertation: University of Helsinki.

Hayes, Bruce (1982) Extrametricality and English Stress. *LI* 13: 227–76.

Hayes, Bruce (1986) Assimilation as Spreading in Toba Batak. *LI* 17: 467–99.

Hayes, Bruce (1989) Compensatory Lengthening in Moraic Phonology. *LI* 20: 253–306.

Hayes, Bruce (1995) *Metrical Stress Theory: Principles and Case Studies*. Chicago, IL and London: University of Chicago Press.

Herzallah, Ruqayyah (1990) *Aspects of Palestinian Arabic Phonology: A Non-Linear Approach.* Doctoral dissertation: Cornell University.

Horwood, Graham (2001) Anti-faithfulness and Subtractive Morphology. Ms., Rutgers University. [ROA-466]

Hsieh, Feng-fan (2005) Tonal Chain-shifts as Anti-neutralization-induced Tone Sandhi. In Sudha Arunachalam, Tatjana Scheffler, Sandhya Sundaresan, and Joshua Taubere (eds) *Proceedings of the 28th Penn Linguistics Colloquium, Penn Working Papers in Linguistics* 11.1, 99–112. Philadelphia, PA: Department of Linguistics, University of Pennsylvania.

Hualde, José (1989) Autosegmental and Metrical Spreading in the Vowel-harmony Systems of Northwestern Spain. *Linguistics* 27: 773–805.

Hualde, José (1990) Compensatory Lengthening in Friulian. *Probus: International Journal of Romance Linguistics* 2: 31–46.

Hudson, Grover (1974) The Representation of Non-productive Alternation. In J. Anderson and C. Jones (eds) *Historical Linguistics*, 203–29. Amsterdam: North-Holland.

Hyman, Larry (1985) *A Theory of Phonological Weight.* Dordrecht: Foris.

Ingram, David (1974) Phonological Rules in Young Children. *Journal of Child Language* 1: 49–64.

Ito, Junko (1982) The Syllable Structure of Russian. Ms., University of Massachusetts, Amherst.

Ito, Junko (1988) *Syllable Theory in Prosodic Phonology*. New York: Garland Publishing. [1986 Doctoral dissertation, University of Massachusetts, Amherst.]

Ito, Junko (1989) A Prosodic Theory of Epenthesis. *NLLT* 7: 217–259.

Ito, Junko and Mester, Armin (2004) Morphological Contrast and Merger: Ranuki in Japanese. *Journal of Japanese Linguistics* 20: 1–18.

Ito, Junko and Mester, Armin (2007) Systemic Markedness and Faithfulness. *CLS* 39: 665–89.

Ito, Junko, Mester, Armin, and Padgett, Jaye (1995) Licensing and Redundancy: Underspecification in Optimality Theory. *LI* 26: 571–614.

Jacobs, Haike (2000) The Revenge of the Uneven Trochee: Latin Main Stress, Metrical Constituency, Stress-related Phenomena and OT. In A. Lahiri (ed.) *Analogy, Leveling, Markedness*, 333–52. Berlin: Mounton de Gruyter.

Jaker, Alex (2006) Split Subject Agreement and Morphological Typology. Ms., Stanford University.

Jaworski, Michał (1986) *Podręczna Gramatyka Języka Polskiego*. Warszawa: Wydawnictwa Szkolne i Pedagogiczne.

Kager, René (1995) Metrical Theory of Word Stress. In John A. Goldsmith (ed.) *The Handbook of Phonological Theory*, 367–402. Cambridge, MA: Blackwell.

Kager, René (1996) On Affix Allomorphy and Syllable Counting. In Ursula Kleinhenz (ed.) *Interfaces in Phonology*, 155–71. Berlin: Akademie Verlag. (Studia Grammatica 41.)

Kager, René (1999a) Surface Opacity of Metrical Structure in Optimality Theory. In B. Hermans and M. van Oostendorp (eds) *The Derivational Residue in Phonological Optimality Theory*, 207–45. Amsterdam: John Benjamins.

Kager, René (1999b) *Optimality Theory*. Cambridge: Cambridge University Press.

Karlsson, Fred (1999) *Finnish: An Essential Grammar*. London and New York: Routledge.

Katada, F. (1990) On the Representation of Moras: Evidence from a Language Game. *LI* 21: 641–46.

Kaye, Jonathan (1974) Opacity and Recoverability in Phonology. *Canadian Journal of Linguistics* 19: 134–49.

Kaye, Jonathan (1975) A Functional Explanation for Rule Ordering in Phonology. *CLS: Papers from the Parasession on Functionalism*, 244–52. Chicago, IL: Chicago Linguistics Society.

Kaze, Jeffrey (1989) *Metaphony in Italian and Spanish Dialects Revisited*. Doctoral dissertation: University of Illinois, Urbana-Champaign.

Kean, M.-L. (1974) The Strict Cycle in Phonology. *LI* 5, 179–203.

Keating, P. A. (1988) Palatals as Complex Segments: X-ray Evidence. *UCLA Working Papers in Phonetics* 69: 77–91.

Keer, Edward (2000) *Geminates, The OCP and Faithfulness*. Doctoral dissertation: Rutgers University.

Kenstowicz, Michael (1981) The Metrical Structure of Arabic Accent. Ms., University of Illinois.

Kenstowicz, Michael (1996) Base-Identity and Uniform Exponence: Alternatives to Cyclicity. In J. Durand and B. Laks (eds) *Current Trends in Phonology: Models and Methods*, 363–94. [ROA-103]

Kenstowicz, Michael (2005) Paradigmatic Uniformity and Contrast. In L. J. Downing, T. A. Hall, and R. Raffelsiefen (eds) *Paradigms in Phonological Theory*, 145–69. Oxford: Oxford University Press.

Kenstowicz, Michael and Kisseberth, Charles (1979) *Generative Phonology: Description and Theory*. New York: Academic Press.

Keyser, Samuel J. and Kiparsky, Paul (1984) Syllable Structure in Finnish Phonology. In Mark Aronoff and Richard T. Oehrle (eds) *Language Sound Structure*, 7–31. Cambridge, MA and London: MIT Press.

King, Robert (1969) Push Chains and Drag Chains. *Glossa* 3.1: 3–21.

Kingston, John and Diehl, Randy L. (1994) Phonetic Knowledge. *Language* 70: 419–54.

Kiparsky, Paul (1971) Historical Linguistics. In W. O. Dingwall (ed.) *A Survey of Linguistic Science*, 576–642. College Park, MA: University of Maryland Linguistics Program.

Kiparsky, Paul (1973) Abstractness, Opacity and Global Rules. In Osamu Fujimura (ed.) *Three Dimensions in Linguistic Theory*, 57–86. Tokyo: TEC.

Kiparsky, Paul (1982) *Explanation in Phonology*. Dordrecht: Foris.

Kiparsky, Paul (1993) Blocking in Non-Derived Environments. In S. Hargus and E. Kaisse (eds) *Studies in Lexical Phonology*, 277–313. San Diego, CA: Academic Press.

Kiparsky, Paul (1997) LP and OT. Handout from Cornell Linguistic Institute, July.

Kiparsky, Paul (2000) Opacity and Cyclicity. *The Linguistic Review* 17: 351–67.

Kiparsky, Paul (2002) Syllables and Moras in Arabic. In C. Fery and R. Vijver (eds) *The Syllable in Optimality Theory*, 147–82. Cambridge: Cambridge University Press.

Kiparsky, Paul (to appear) *Paradigm Effects and Opacity*. Stanford: CSLI.

Kirchner, Robert (1996) Synchronic Chain Shifts in Optimality Theory. *LI* 27: 341–50.

Kisseberth, Charles (1976) The Interaction of Phonological Rules and the Polarity of Language. In Andreas Koutsoudas (ed.) *The Application and Ordering of Phonological Rules*, 41–54. The Hague: Mounton.

Kisseberth, Charles and Abasheikh, Mohammad I. (1974) A Case of Systematic Avoidance of Homonyms. *Studies in the Linguistic Sciences* 4.1: 107–24.

Kochetov, Alexei (2001) *Production, Perception, and Emergent Phonotactic Patterns: A Case of Contrastive Palatalization*. Doctoral dissertation: University of Toronto.

Kubozono, Haruo (2001) On the Markedness of Diphthongs. *Kobe Papers in Linguistics* 3: 60–73.

Kurisu, Suzuki (1998) *A Typological Investigation of Dissimilation*. Doctoral dissertation: University of Arizona.

Labov, William (1994) *Principles of Linguistic Change: Internal Factors*. Oxford: Blackwell Publishers.

Ladefoged, Peter and Maddieson, Ian (1996) *The Sounds of the World's Languages*. Oxford: Blackwell.

Lass, R. (1999) Phonology and Morphology. In *The Cambridge History of the English Language* vol. III: 1476 to 1776, 56–186. Cambridge: Cambridge University Press.

Lehtinen, Meri (1967) *Basic Course in Finnish*. Bloomington, IN: Indiana University Publications, Uralic and Altaic Series.

Leinonen-Davies, Eeva (1988) Assessing the Functional Adequacy of Children's Phonological Systems. *Clinical Linguistics and Phonetics* 2.4: 257–70.

Liao, Wei-wen Roger (2007) The Morpho-syntactic Mismatch in Taiwanese Negation Prefixes as a Consequence of Contrast Preservation. Ms., University of Southern California.

Liberman, Mark and Prince, Alan (1977) On Stress and Linguistic Rhythm. *LI* 8: 249–336.

Lindblom, Björn (1986) Phonetic Universals in Vowel Systems. In John J. Ohala and Jeri J. Jaeger (eds) *Experimental Phonology*, 13–44. Orlando, FL: Academic Press.

Lindblom, Björn (1990) Explaining Phonetic Variation: A Sketch of the H&H Theory. In William J. Hardcastle and Alain Marchal (eds) *Speech Production and Speech Modeling* 403–39. Dordrecht: Kluwer.

Lombardi, Linda (2001) Why Place and Voice are Different: Constraint-specific Alternations in Optimality Theory. In Linda Lombardi (ed.) *Segmental Phonology in Optimality Theory: Constraints and Representations*, 13–45. Cambridge: Cambridge University Press.

Luick, K. (1914) *Historische Grammatik der englischen Sprache*, 2 Vols. – 1921 [1964]. Stuttgart: Tauchnitz.

Lunt, Horace G. (2001) *Old Church Slavonic Grammar*. Berlin and New York: Mouton de Gruyter.

Łubowicz, Anna (2002) Derived Environment Effects in Optimality Theory. *Lingua* 112: 243–80.

Łubowicz, Anna (2003) *Contrast Preservation in Phonological Mappings*. Doctoral dissertation. Amherst, MA: University of Massachusetts, Amherst. [Available on Rutgers Optimality Archive, ROA-554.]

Łubowicz, Anna (2004) Counter-Feeding Opacity As a Chain Shift Effect. In G. Garding and M. Tsujimura (eds) *WCCFL* 22: 315–27. Somerville, MA: Cascadilla Press..

Łubowicz, Anna (2007) Paradigmatic Contrast in Polish. *Journal of Slavic Linguistics* 15.2: 229–62.

Łubowicz, Anna, Go, Nathan, Huang, Nancy, and McDonald, Sara (2007) Nickname Formation in Polish: The Case of Allomorph Selection. In R. Compton, M. Goledzinowska, and U. Savchenko (eds) *Proceedings of the 15th Conference on Formal Approaches to Slavic Linguistics*, 196–209. Ann Arbor, MI: Michigan Slavic Publications.

Maclagan, Margaret and Hay, Jen (2004) The Rise and Rise of New Zealand English DRESS. *Proceedings of the 10th Australian International Conference on Speech Science and Technology*: 183–88.

Martinet, André (1952) Function, Structure and Sound Change. *Word* 8: 1–32.

Martinet, André (1955) *Economie des changements phonétiques*. Berne: Francke.

Mascaró, J. (1976) Catalan Phonology and the Phonological Cycle. Ph.D. dissertation: Massachusetts Institute of Technology.

Mascaró, Joan (1996) External Allomorphy as Emergence of the Unmarked. In Jacques Durand and Bernard Laks (eds) *Current Trends in Phonology: Models and Methods*, 473–83. Salford, Manchester: European Studies Research Institute, University of Salford. (Reprinted in McCarthy 2004.)

McCarthy, John J. (1993) A Case of Surface Constraint Violation. In Carole Paradis and Darlene LaCharité (eds) *Constraint-Based Theories in Multilinear Phonology*, special issue of *Canadian Journal of Linguistics* 38: 169–95.

McCarthy, John J. (1997) Process-specific Constraints in Optimality Theory. *LI* 28: 231–51.

McCarthy, John J. (1999) Sympathy and Phonological Opacity. *Phonology* 16: 331–99.

McCarthy, John J. (2003a) Sympathy, Cumulativity, and the Duke-of-York Gambit. In Caroline Féry and Ruben van de Vijver (eds) *The Syllable in Optimality Theory*, 23–76. Cambridge: Cambridge University Press.

McCarthy, John J. (2003b) Comparative Markedness. *Theoretical Linguistics* 29: 1–51.

McCarthy, John J. (2003c) OT Constraints are Categorical. *Phonology* 20, 75–138.

McCarthy, John J. (2004) *A Thematic Guide to Optimality Theory*. Cambridge: Cambridge University Press.

McCarthy, John J. (2005) Optimal Paradigms. In Laura Downing, Tracy Alan Hall and Renate Raffelsiefen (eds) *Paradigms in Phonological Theory*. Oxford: Oxford University Press.

McCarthy, John J. (2007) *Hidden Generalizations: Phonological Opacity in Optimality Theory*. London: Equinox.

McCarthy, John J. and Prince, Alan (1990a) Foot and Word in Prosodic Morphology: The Arabic Broken Plural. *NLLT* 8: 209–83.

McCarthy, John J. and Prince, Alan (1990b) Prosodic Morphology and Templatic Morphology. In Mushira Eid and John McCarthy (eds) *Perspectives on Arabic Linguistics II*, 1–54. Amsterdam and Philadelphia, PA: John Benjamins.

McCarthy, John J. and Prince, Alan (1993) Generalized Alignment. In G. E. Booij and J. van Marle (eds) *Yearbook of Morphology*, 79–153. Kluwer: Dordrecht.

McCarthy, John J. and Prince, Alan (1995) Faithfulness and Reduplicative Identity. In J. Beckman, L. Walsh Dickey, and S. Urbanczyk (eds) *University of Massachusetts Occasional Papers 18: Papers in Optimality Theory*, 249–384. Amherst, MA: GLSA.

McCarthy, John J. and Prince, Alan (1996) *Prosodic Morphology 1986*. Technical Report #32, Rutgers University Center for Cognitive Science.

McCawley, James (1964) The Morphophonemics of the Finnish Noun. Ms., Massachusetts Institute of Technology. [Mechanical Translation Group, Research Laboratory of Electronics.]

McLaughlin, John E. (1984) A Revised Approach to Southern Paiute Phonology. *Kansas Working Papers in Linguistics* 9: 47–79.

Mester, R. Armin (1994) The Quantitative Trochee in Latin. *NLLT* 12: 1–62.

Mester, R. Armin and Padgett, Jaye (1994) Directional Syllabification in Generalized Alignment. In Jason Merchant, Jaye Padgett, and Rachel Walker (eds) *Phonology at Santa Cruz* [*PASC*] vol. 3: 79–85.

Michelson, Karin (1989) Invisibility: Vowels Without a Timing Slot in Mohawk. In Donna Gerdts and Karin Michelson (eds) *Theoretical Perspectives on Native American Languages*, 38–69. Albany, NY: SUNY.

Miglio, Viola and Morén, Bruce (2003) Merger Avoidance and Lexical Reconstruction. In D. Eric Holt (ed.) *Optimality Theory and Language Change*, 191–228. The Netherlands: Kluwer Academic Publishers.

Minkova, Donka and Stockwell, Robert (2003) English Vowel Shifts and "Optimal" Diphthongs: Is there a Logical Link? In D. Eric Holt (ed.) *Optimality Theory and Language Change*, 169–90. The Netherlands : Kluwer Academic Publishers.

Mitchell, T. F. (1975) *Principles of Firthian Linguistics*. London: Longman.

Morén, Bruce (2001) *Distinctiveness, Coercion and Sonority: A Unified Theory of Weight*. New York: Routledge.

Moreton, Elliott (1996/1999) Non-Computable Functions in Optimality Theory. Ms., University of Massachusetts, Amherst. [ROA-364]

Moreton, Elliott and Smolensky, Paul (2002) Typological Consequences of Local Constraint Conjunction. In L. Mikkelsen and C. Potts (eds) *WCCFL* 21: 306–19.

Ní Chiosáin, Máire (1991) *Topics in the Phonology of Irish.* Doctoral dissertation. Amherst, MA: University of Massachusetts, Amherst.

Ní Chiosáin, Máire and Padgett, Jaye (2010) Contrast, Comparison Sets, and the Perceptual Space. In Steve Parker (ed.) *Phonological Argumentation: Essays on Evidence and Motivation*, 103–21. London: Equinox.

Oostendorp, Mark van (1998) Opacity in Allomorphy: The Case of Aalst Dutch. GLOW (Generative Linguistics in the Old World), April 1998.

Padgett, Jaye (1997) Candidates as Systems: Saussure Lives! Handout from Hopkins Optimality Workshop.

Padgett, Jaye (2000) The Role of Contrast in Russian (Historical) Phonology. Handout of talk given at Massachusetts Institute of Technology, May 12.

Padgett, Jaye (2001) Contrast Dispersion and Russian Palatalization. In Elizabeth Hume and Keith Johnson (eds) *The Role of Speech Perception in Phonology*, 187–218. San Diego, CA: Academic Press.

Padgett, Jaye (2003) Contrast and Post-velar Fronting in Russian. *NLLT* 21.1: 39–87.

Padgett, Jaye and Zygis, Marzena (2007) The Evolution of Sibilants in Polish and Russian. *Journal of Slavic Linguistics* 15.2: 291–324.

Parkinson, Frederick B. (1996) *The Representation of Vowel Height in Phonology*. Doctoral dissertation: Ohio State University.

Parrell, Ben (2007) Vowel Length and Final Devoicing in Friulian: A Case of Contrast Preservation. Ms., University of Southern California.

Paster, Mary (2005) Subcategorization vs. Output Optimization in Syllable-counting Allomorphy. In John Alderete, Chung-hye Han, and Alexei Kochetov (eds) *WCCFL* 24: 326–33. Somerville, MA: Cascadilla Proceedings Project.

Pater, Joe (1999) Austronesian Nasal Substitution and other NC̥ Effects. In Rene Kager, Harry van der Hulst, and Wim Zonneveld (eds) *The Prosody-Morphology Interface* 310–43. Cambridge: Cambridge University Press. [ROA-160]

Pater, Joe (2000) Nonuniformity in English Stress: The Role of Ranked and Lexically Specific Constraints. *Phonology* 17.2: 237–74.

Piggott, Glyne L. (1988) Prenasalization and Feature Representation. *NELS* 19: 345–52. Amherst, MA: GLSA.

Piggott, Glyne L. (1995) Epenthesis and Syllable Weight. *NLLT* 13: 283–326.

Piggott, Glyne L. (1998) Foot Form and the Parsing of Weightless Syllables. In M. Gruber, D. Higgins, K. Olson, and T. Wysocki (eds) *Papers from the 34th Regional Meeting of the Chicago Linguistic Society* (CLS 34, Main Session), 315–32. Chicago, IL: Chicago Linguistics Society.

Piggott, Glyne L. (1999) At the Right Edge of Words. *The Linguistic Review* 16: 143–85.

Prince, Alan and Smolensky, Paul (1993) Optimality Theory: Constraint Interaction in Generative Grammar. Report RUCCS TR-2. Rutgers University, New Brunswick, NJ. [2004 edn Malden, MA; Oxford, UK; Carlton, Australia: Blackwell.]

Puppel, Stanisław, Nawrocka-Fisiak, Jadwiga, and Krassowska, Halina (1977) *A Handbook of Polish Pronunciation for English Learners*. Warsaw: Państwowe Wydawnictwo Naukowe.

Qafisheh, Hamdi A. (1977) *A Short Reference Grammar of Gulf Arabic*. Tucson, AZ: University of Arizona Press.

Rebrus, Péter and Törkenczy, Miklós (2005) Uniformity and Contrast in the Hungarian Verbal Paradigm. In L. J. Downing, T. A. Hall, and R. Raffelsiefen (eds) *Paradigms in Phonological Theory*, 263–65. Oxford: Oxford University Press.

Repetti, Lori (1992) Vowel Length in Northern Italian Dialects. *Probus: International Journal of Romance Linguistics* 4: 155–82.

Repetti, Lori (1994) Degenerate Syllables in Friulian. *LI* 25: 186–93.
Repetti, Lori (2000) *Phonological Theory and the Dialects of Italy*. Amsterdam and Philadelphia, PA: John Benjamins.
Revithiadou, Anthi (1999) *Headmost Accent Wins*. Doctoral dissertation: HIL/Leiden University. [ROA-388]
Rice, Keren and Avery, Peter (1993) Segmental Complexity and the Structure of Inventories. In C. Dyck (ed.) *Toronto Working Papers in Linguistics* 12: 131–54.
Riggs, Daylen (2008) Contrast Preservation in the Yupik Languages. In Rebecca Colavin, Kathryn Cooke, Kathryn Davidson, Shin Fukuda, and Alex del Giudice (eds) *Proceedings of the Thirty-Seventh Western Conference on Linguistics, WECOL 2007*, 217–34, vol. 18.
Rosenthall, Sam and van der Hulst, Harry (1999) Weight-by-position by Position. *NLLT* 17: 499–540.
Rospond, Stanisław (1971) *Gramatyka historyczna języka polskiego*. Warszawa: PWN.
Rothstein, Robert A. (1993) Polish. In Bernard Comrie and Greville G. Corbett (eds) *The Slavonic Languages*, 686–758. London and New York: Routledge.
Rubach, Jerzy (1981) *Cyclic Phonology and Palatalization in Polish and English*. Warszawa: Wydawnictwa Uniwersytetu Warszawskiego.
Rubach, Jerzy (1984) *Cyclic and Lexical Phonology: The Structure of Polish*. Dordrecht: Foris.
Rubach, Jerzy (1996) Nonsyllabic Analysis of Voice Assimilation in Polish. *LI* 27: 69–110.
Rubach, Jerzy (2003) Polish Palatalization in Derivational Optimality Theory. *Lingua* 113: 197–237.
Rubach, Jerzy and Booij, Geert (1990) Edge of Constituent Effects in Polish. *NLLT* 8: 427–63.
Rubach, Jerzy and Booij, Geert (2001) Allomorphy in Optimality Theory: Polish Iotation. *Language* 77: 26–60.
Sanders, Nathan (2003) *Opacity and Sound Change in the Polish Lexicon*. Doctoral dissertation: University of California, Santa Cruz.
Sapir, Edward (1930) Southern Paiute, a Shoshonean Language. *Proceedings of the American Academy of Arts and Sciences* 65: 1–296.
Saussure, Ferdinand de. (1983) *Course in General Linguistics*. Charles Bally and Albert Sechehaye (eds). Translation by Roy Harris. La Salle, IL: Open Court. [1916]
Schendl, Herbert and Ritt, Nikolaus (2002) Of Vowel Shifts Great, Small, Long and Short. *Language Sciences* 24: 409–21.
Schmidt, Deborah Schlindwein (1996) Vowel Raising in Basaá: A Synchronic Chain Shift. *Phonology* 13: 239–67.
Selkirk, Elisabeth (1981) Epenthesis and Degenerate Syllables in Cairene Arabic. In Hagit Borer and Youssef Aoun (eds) *Theoretical Issues in the Grammar of Semitic Languages: MIT Working Papers in Linguistics* 3: 209–32. Cambridge, MA: Massachusetts Institute of Technology.
Shaaban, Kassim Ali (1977) *The Phonology of Omani Arabic*. Doctoral dissertation: University of Texas, Austin.
Sherer, Tim D. (1994) *Prosodic Phonotactics*. Doctoral dissertation. Amherst, MA: University of Massachusetts, Amherst. [Available on Rutgers Optimality Archive, ROA-54.]
Siegel, Dorothy (1974) *Topics in English Morphophonology*. Doctoral dissertation: Massachusetts Institute of Technology.
Smolensky, Paul (1993) Harmony, Markedness, and Phonological Activity, Handout of talk presented at Rutgers Optimality Workshop 1, October 23, New Brunswick, NJ. [ROA-87]
Smolensky, Paul (1997) Constraint Interaction in Generative Grammar II: Local Conjunction or Random Rules in Universal Grammar. Handout of talk presented at Hopkins Optimality Theory Workshop, Baltimore, MA.

Steriade, Donca (1995) Underspecification and Markedness. In John A. Goldsmith (ed.) *The Handbook of Phonological Theory*, 114–74. Cambridge, MA: Blackwell.

Steriade, Donca (1997) Lexical Conservatism and its Analysis. Ms., University of California, Los Angeles.

Steriade, Donca (2000) Paradigm Uniformity and the Phonetics-Phonology Boundary. In Michael B. Broe and Janet B. Pierrehumbert (eds) *Papers in Laboratory Phonology* 5: 131–34. Cambridge, UK and New York, NY: Cambridge University Press.

Struijke, Caro (2001) *Existential Faithfulness: A Study of Reduplicative TETU, Feature Movement, and Dissimilation.* Doctoral dissertation: University of Maryland, College Park.

Styczek, Irena (1973) *Badania Eksperymentalne Spirantów Polskich s, š, ś ze Stanowiska Fizjologii i Patologii Mowy.* Wrocław: Wydawnictwo Polskiej Akademii Nauk.

Szober, Stanisław (1969) *Gramatyka Języka Polskiego.* Warszawa: Państwowe Wydawnictwo Naukowe.

Tessier, Anne-Michelle (2004) Input "Clusters" and Contrast Preservation in OT. In Vineeta Chand, Ann Kelleher, Angelo J. Rodríguez, and Benjamin Schmeiser (eds) *WCCFL* 23: 101–14. Somerville, MA: Cascadilla Press.

Tranel, Bernard (1996) French Liaison and Elision Revisited: A Unified Account Within Optimality Theory. In Claudia Parodi, Carlos Quicoli, Mario Saltarelli, and Maria Luisa Zubizarreta (eds) *Aspects of Romance Linguistics*, 433–55. Washington, DC: Georgetown University Press. [ROA-15]

Tranel, Bernard (1998) Suppletion and OT: On the Issue of the Syntax/phonology Interaction. In E. Curtis *et al.* (eds) *WCCFL* 16: 415–29. Stanford, CA: CSLI.

Trimingham, J. Spencer (1946) *Sudan Colloquial Arabic.* Oxford: Oxford University Press.

Trubetzkoy, N. Sergeevich (1971) *Principles of Phonology*. Berkeley, CA: University of California Press. [1939]

Trudgill, P., Gordon, E., and Lewis, G. (1998) New Dialect Formation and Southern Hemisphere English: The New Zealand Short Front Vowels. *Journal of Sociolinguistics* 2: 35–51.

Ultan, Russell (1970) Some Sources of Consonant Gradation. In *Working Papers on Language Universals* 2, 1–30. Stanford, CA: Stanford University, Committee on Linguistics.

Urbanczyk, Suzanne (1998) Avoidance of the Marked. Ms., University of British Columbia and University of Victoria. [ROA-286]

Urbanczyk, Suzanne (1999) A-templatic Reduplication in Halq'eméylem. In Kimary Shahin, Susan Blake, and Eun-Sook Kim (eds) *WCCFL* 17: 655–69. Stanford, CA: CSIL Publications.

West, P. (1999) The Extent of Coarticulation of English Liquids: An Acoustic and Articulatory Study. *International Congress of Phonetics Sciences* 99.3: 1901–1904.

Wierzchowska, Bożena (1971) *Wymowa Polska.* Warszawa: Państwowe Zakłady Wydawnictw Szkolnych.

Wilson, Colin (2001) Consonant Cluster Neutralization and Targeted Constraints. *Phonology* 18: 147–97.

Wolf, Matthew (2008) *Optimal Interleaving: Serial Phonology-Morphology Interaction in a Constraint-Based Model.* Doctoral dissertation: University of Massachusetts, Amherst.

Wolf, Matthew and McCarthy, John J. (2009) Less than Zero: Correspondence and the Null Output. In Curt Rice (ed.) *Modeling Ungrammaticality in Optimality Theory*, 17–66. London: Equinox Publishing. [Earlier version available as ROA-722.]

Yip, Moira (1988) The Obligatory Contour Principle and Phonological Rules: A Loss of Identity. *LI* 19.1: 65–100.

Yip, Moira (2004) Phonological Markedness and Allomorph Selection in Zahao. *Language and Linguistics* 5.4: 969–1001.

Zec, Draga (1988) *Sonority Constraints on Prosodic Structure*. Doctoral dissertation: Stanford University.

Zoll, Cheryl (1997) Conflicting Directionality. *Phonology* 14: 263–86.

Index

www.ingramcontent.com/pod-product-compliance
Lightning Source LLC
La Vergne TN
LVHW011204090826
844660LV00058B/266